Anthony & Wendy
from Donnie
(here in disguise!)
6 March 1997.

THE REAL JESUS

THE REAL JESUS

BENEDICT CLEMENT

NEW MILLENNIUM
292 Kennington Road, London SE11 4LD.

Copyright © 1997 Benedict Clement

All rights reserved. No part of this publication may be reproduced in any form, except for the purposes of review, without prior written permission from the copyright owner.

Printed and bound by Arm Crown Ltd. Uxbridge Road, Middx.
Issued by New Millennium*
ISBN 1 85845 112 4
*An imprint of The Professional Authors' & Publishers' Association

Contents

		Page
Foreword		1
Chapter I	The Legacy of Paul	5
Chapter II	The Background	11
Chapter III	Gospel Texts – Have the Originals Survived?	23
Chapter IV	The Gospels – Origins and Accuracy	31
Chapter V	The Gospel Miracles	53
Chapter VI	The Nativity – Early Years and Mission	63
Chapter VII	Crucifixion – Resurrection or Resuscitation?	85
Chapter VIII	Jesus: Teacher of Righteousness	109
Chapter IX	The Church in the Third Millennium	123
Appendix	For rapid reference	
	Map	134
	Persons, Places and Subjects	135
	Dates	149
Bibliography		153
Index		157

Foreword

THE TRUTH is that we know very little for certain about Jesus, the figure on whom Christianity is founded. We know that he was born between BC 10 and 5 AD - a period of fourteen years; we know that he was executed by crucifixion (although even that has been challenged) somewhere around the year 33 AD. Most scholars prefer an earlier rather than a later date for his birth, which means that he would have been about forty when he died. Of these forty years the four gospels in the New Testament provide us with much valuable information about the last three of them at the most, with two very different and equally unreliable accounts of his birth and earliest years. But for the greatest part of his life all four gospels are equally silent.

To most people Jesus is known as "Jesus Christ", using the word "Christ" as if it were a surname. The word "Christ" means "the Anointed One" and is the Greek equivalent of the Jewish title "Messiah", which also means "the Anointed One." In the days of Jesus, kings, prophets and priests were all anointed, and the term applied to Jesus is thus open to a number of interpretations.

Until the middle of the nineteenth century there were few in the Christian world who were bold enough to challenge the accepted opinion that the gospels give an accurate, indeed infallible, description of the life of Jesus. More recently the historical validity of the gospels has been questioned. Nevertheless they have been used as the basis for many a word-portrait of Jesus. Although he is nowadays often presented as a normal human being he is accepted by the majority of Christians as "The Lord", albeit often with neither the theological nor the philosophical training to have any clear idea what the term means, with the result that each creates a Jesus of his or her own imagining, adapted to the needs of each individual. It is an element of human nature, more evident in some than others, particularly strong in the young, to feel the need of a hero to adulate and of an ideal to inspire them, be it a pop star or a prophet. Sunday worshippers, especially those in "charismatic" congregations, arms and eyes upraised in apparent ecstasy, believe themselves to be "saved" by Jesus, yet know almost nothing about the man who once lived in Galilee whose name they invoke. They are dazzled by the bright vision of their own creation.

These worshippers are doing what Christians have done for nearly two thousand years: they create an idol and call him Jesus. In the first Christian centuries there was the Jesus idol hewn from Greek philosophy, polished with Jewish tradition; in the Middle Ages there was the Jesus God, so awesome for many that humbler folk needed the more comforting reassurance of his more human Mother; and latterly there is Jesus the merciful healer and gentle teacher, drawn from those of the gospel accounts of his words and deeds selected as best befitting their own personal picture of the Ideal Man.

Throughout the whole of the Christian era, whatever may have been the form in which Jesus was portrayed, the conviction for many has proved so strong that not only were they prepared to die for him, not only were they prepared to give up every other ambition in order to serve him, but even to suffer for him the most appalling tortures – the lions of Nero, the flames of the Inquisition, the rack of the Reformers – and, in order to serve him in the manner they believed he wished to be served, to inflict the most appalling tortures on those whose picture of him differed from their own. It was not the real Jesus they followed but a Jesus of their own imagining, the Jesus that corresponded either to the image they had been brought up to believe in or the image that their personal needs had created. Alas! with the best will in the world, on this side of the grave we cannot know the real Jesus. We are left to conceive him as we will.

But a real Jesus did once live – of that there can be no reasonable doubt – and Christianity, in all its varied forms, exists because he lived. In every village in Europe and in many places beyond there is today a monument - often an old and imposing monument - that owes its existence solely to the fact that Jesus once lived in Galilee. Prominent in towns and cities are examples of some of the world's finest and most magnificent architecture, buildings which would not have been conceived had Jesus not lived - the parish churches and cathedrals, abbey ruins and minsters - all are statements by their builders of their belief in Jesus, uncritically conceived.

In recent years many attempts have been made to discover what more we can learn of the real Jesus from historical and archaeological sources. The result has been the production of a great variety of different pictures, some more probable than others, but none completely convincing or satisfactory. The same evidence in different hands may give rise to a wide divergence of conclusions. Inevitably it is that period of Jesus's life, the one to three years of his mission immediately preceding his crucifixion, that short period of his life covered by the gospels, that is presented. Little attention, if any, is given to the many years of his life about which the gospels remain silent.

This book does not claim to give answers which no one else can give. It has two objectives: first, to discuss how far we can accept the gospels as historical documents, and second, to suggest what may have happened during those many unrecorded years. Much will be guesswork. But outside the gospels, and even in them, too, there are pointers to help us guess aright. But how right? Let the Reader be the judge.

Note:
It may be as well to explain here that the use in this book of such words as "Man" and "Mankind", and the cognate pronouns "he", "him", "his", etc., are used to embrace both male and female members the human race. The pronoun used for God is "he" not

because God has a gender but because the English language has no word other than "it" to express an idea without gender, and "it" seems hardly suitable for God. Jesus lived in a paternalistic society and used the language and images of his day. Had he lived in England in the third millennium he might have used different images but, as he was a realist, this is open to doubt.

CHAPTER I
THE LEGACY OF PAUL

The evolution of Christianity and its spread throughout the Roman Empire was due more to the missionary work of S.Paul the apostle than to any of the original followers of Jesus. In fact, it is often said that Paul invented Christianity – and in doing so he "invented" a Jesus that was very different from the Palestinian Jewish Teacher in whose name he preached and wrote. It is largely due to his efforts that, in the countries of modern Europe which together once formed medieval Christendom, Christianity has survived, as the dominant religion, for nearly two thousand years.

During the greater period of Paul's missionary work the gospels did not exist, at least not as we have them today. There may have been some written records available to the few, but for the most part those to whom Paul preached had no other source of knowledge about the life and teaching of Jesus than what he told them. There was no accepted creed, no formulated dogmas. Paul was a man of great intelligence, a man of indomitable perseverance and resolve. He had his own ideas in which he was totally absorbed, ideas which he believed it was his God-ordained duty to spread. To the strength of his conviction must be attributed the signal success of his efforts. As the result of Paul's determination, Christianity has remained enchained by his doctrine for two thousand years, and the official, orthodox view of who and what Jesus was remains firmly founded on his teaching.

It is important to understand what happened – as far as can be known.

The crucifixion of Jesus took place in the Spring of AD33, or very near that date. After his resuscitation (as explained in Chapter VII) Jesus did not remain long in Palestine, but left his most faithful disciples, whom he appointed "apostles", to continue to preach his message. These remained together for a while, with other followers of Jesus. They were a small group of men and women who gathered together for prayer under the guidance of James, a cousin of Jesus (usually called his "brother"). At that time there was no church organization, but in a sense James might be called the first Christian bishop, the bishop of Jerusalem.

These followers of Jesus, most, if not all, Essenes, and still calling themselves Jews, were considered heretics by the strict Pharisees, of whom a certain Saul was one. He had studied under Gamaliel, a learned Jewish teacher of the orthodox school. Saul was violently opposed to these new groups of Jesus's heretical followers. Because of his animosity towards them he was specially commissioned to help suppress their increase among the scattered Jewish communities. There was a report of such a group forming in Damascus, the capital of Syria, and Saul was sent there to deal with it. This happened some two years after the crucifixion, probably in AD35.

Saul was an energetic and very intelligent and determined man, but he suffered from some affliction. What it was we do not know; it is often thought it was epilepsy. This would explain what happened when he was on the way to Damascus. He had what in modern parlance is called "a religious experience". He may have had some sort of fit, and with his mind full of his purpose imagined Jesus spoke to him. The "fit" may have appeared to be a sign from God of his anger at the work Saul was doing. Whatever happened, Saul was convinced that Jesus had come to him and rebuked him. Temporarily blinded, he went on to Damascus, recovered his sight and, believing himself called by Jesus, was converted and baptized, and changed his name to Paul – why, we do not know. The name seems to have come from the Latin *paulus*, small, and may have been an act of humility. "Saul" means "the wanted one", a name that one can easily understand parents giving to a long-awaited son, but one of which Paul may have considered himself no longer worthy.

It was common knowledge among the first Christians that Jesus had survived the crucifixion, and to the popular mind this meant "resurrection" from the dead. Having "seen" Jesus, Saul was convinced that Jesus had indeed risen from the dead – and on that assumption he built the theology he would henceforth preach during his missionary journeys. It is not impossible that Jesus was at that time in Damascus, well away from Jerusalem, protected by the group of Essenes Saul had set out to denounce: if so, then it may be that he did in truth meet Jesus and receive from him a commission to preach on his behalf. He could also have met him during his period of "initiation", which, if arranged by the Essenes, would normally have been for three years.

He eventually went back to Jerusalem, and from there set out on his missions which are described in great detail in the New Testament, in the Acts of the Apostles and to some extent in his own letters.

Paul does not seem to have been very popular with the Christians of Jerusalem. They had known Jesus; Paul, their former persecutor, was something of an upstart, and there was friction between him and them. It must indeed have been upsetting for those who had known Jesus personally to have Paul suggesting, through the preaching of his own ideas, that he knew him better than they did.

Paul's theology – based on the theory that God had to be appeased by sacrifices – was no new idea. It was a belief common to many primitive religions, and one that formed part of Jewish belief and practice, and Paul was to some extent applying to Jesus what he had learnt from Gamaliel. Jesus was the supreme sacrificial victim, who, as the Son of God, was the one and only sacrificial victim sufficient enough, in God's eyes, to atone for the sins of all mankind. Paul believed that the resurrection proved that Jesus was the incarnate son of God, sacrificed on the cross to atone for the sins of mankind – for the "original sin" we all inherit from Adam, and for the individual sins we each commit, that through the blood of Jesus those who are baptized in his name would enjoy eternal bliss in the future life, Jesus's resurrection having overcome death. Conversely, the truth of the resurrection was necessary to prove that Jesus did indeed fulfil the role of acceptable sacrificial victim which Paul had allotted to him. The two "truths" were inextricably linked, each depending upon the other.

From this doctrine evolved the belief that the debt having been paid by Jesus, all who accepted him would inherit bliss in the world to come. This teaching was naturally especially popular with the slaves and suppressed peoples of the Roman Empire who had little to look forward to in this life; and many were converted, many died in the belief that their death in this world would be followed by bliss in the next.

Around this doctrine other tenets of the creed were formulated, logically inferred conclusions of syllogisms based on premises invented by Paul. Since future bliss, which depended upon the forgiveness of sins, was in the hands of the Church representing Jesus on earth, the Church had great power – a power that was vastly enhanced when the Emperor Constantine made Christianity the official religion of the Roman Empire (AD326). The Church adopted the centralized organization of the Empire, and eventually, as the Empire waned, replaced it, the bishop of Rome becoming the "Emperor" of the Church, wielding a supreme power that transcended the national boundaries that limited the power of kings and princes.

Most of the doctrines that have evolved throughout the history of the Church have evolved as the outcome of Paul's doctrine of the Incarnation. For example, because Mary, as the mother of Jesus, was considered to be the "mother of God", she had to be completely pure and sinless to be worthy of so great an honour; and if sinless, she was born immaculate and when she died was not subject to the corruption of the flesh (the result of sin), but was assumed bodily and uncorrupted into heaven. Each new doctrine is based logically on the doctrine that precedes it, and all eventually depend on Paul's concept of Jesus, which in its turn was based on the Jewish belief in sacrifice, and elaborated by the Greek philosophy that dominated the way those educated in the current Hellenic culture thought at that time. Much of Paul's teaching was similar, but spiritually superior, to the ideas of Greek mythology, in which gods fathered men by union with human virgins. The similarity was sufficient to make it easily acceptable to the Greek communities to which he preached.

It was not until many years after Paul's death that the Church finally decided which of the gospels were to be accepted as "canonical" – the four gospels we have today. This meant that they were accepted as inspired by God, and therefore infallibly true, which in turn came to mean that every word had to be taken literally. During the "Last Supper" Jesus had said of the bread he broke and distributed to his disciples: "This is my body". It was for this reason that the bread consecrated at the Mass (the celebration of the "Last Supper") was believed to be in truth the body of the incarnate Son of God. From this, in its turn, evolved the doctrine of transubstantiation – a doctrine explained by a philosophy that was essentially Greek in origin – a doctrine which was to have so great an influence on the Church's ritual, and to play so large a part in the disputes of the Reformation. Thus, little by little, as one new doctrine evolved out of another, the Jesus of theology became more and more estranged from the Jesus of history. Although much that has evolved goes beyond what Paul taught it stems from his teaching – it was not part of the teaching of Jesus himself.

Orthodox Christian theology is in truth the legacy of Paul.

In spite of this, something of the character of Jesus himself and of his teaching has survived, and is reflected in the practical lives of many of his followers. It is found in the dedication of such individual followers of Jesus as Mother Teresa and in the work the

Salvation Army, in the private lives of all manner of Christians from Catholic to Quaker.

How much of Jesus's own teaching – how much of Jesus himself – survives in the four gospels? And how much is missing from them? These are the questions we shall try to answer.

Chapter II
The Background

Much of the life of Jesus must inevitably remain a mystery, but if we know something of the world in which he lived we can at least make an informed guess at what he did during the years for which we have no record. We know whereabouts he lived, even if we do not know the exact location; we know within a year or two when he lived, and we know the social and political circumstances that governed the lives of the society to which he belonged.

The main sources for information about the life and work of Jesus are the four gospels. These are traditionally attributed to the four "evangelists" SS.Matthew, Mark, Luke and John. S.Matthew and S. John were two of the specially chosen followers of Jesus, and both were later numbered among the "apostles" who, after the crucifixion, were appointed to continue the work that Jesus had begun. SS. Mark and Luke are not recorded as having been personally involved with Jesus although there are good grounds for supposing that S.Mark was present at some of the events he records, and he was certainly a later companion of S.Peter, nominated by Jesus as his chief disciple. S.Luke is said to have known Jesus's mother, Mary – it is possible. How far the gospels are actually attributable to those whose names they bear is discussed later. Two of the gospels, Matthew and Luke, give an account of the birth of Jesus, and the accuracy of these is also dealt with in a later chapter; and Luke has a brief mention of Jesus at the age of twelve. Unfortunately, except for these stories the gospels make no attempt to tell us anything about the youth and manhood of Jesus before their account of his mission, covering at most the last three years of the near forty Jesus actually lived. The whole picture of Jesus as presented in Christian teaching and tradition is thus based on no more than one thirtieth of his life. On consideration, it seems remarkable that Christians have shown so little curiosity about these hidden years. Can it really be that a man of apparently so charismatic a character, a man of such burning zeal, energy and intelligence, should have remained quietly at home as he worked in his father's carpentry shop in some small village, not considered anyone exceptional by his relatives and neighbours – and then, suddenly, became in the eyes of many of his contemporaries the Anointed One – the Messiah who was to restore to the Jewish people freedom and supremacy among the nations of the world? – and in the eyes of others so great a danger to the security of the establishment as to warrant execution? – for that is how for a few brief days his friends and his enemies regarded him.

To enquire, as far as it is possible, into those hidden years we must know something of Palestine at the time when Jesus lived, and what were the circumstances that could have influenced him and prepared him for the mission he undertook after so many years of obscurity. To do this we have to look for information outside the gospels. To learn about the world in which he lived, its social, religious and political background, we have the historians of both the Romans and the Jews, particularly the historical works of Josephus Flavius, a Jew in favour with the Romans (see below, page 142). We have, too, the writings known as The Dead Sea Scrolls, written mostly shortly before, partly during, the time in which he lived, which give us an insight into the thought and aspirations of the Jewish people around that time. As for the land where Jesus lived, his homeland, it is still there today, richly endowed with archaeological remains. We can check whether what the gospels tell us tallies with independent Roman and Jewish records, with the findings of archaeologists, and with our present knowledge of modern Palestine. Information from all these sources still leaves many questions unanswered, but it helps us to form a reasonably probable picture of the conditions of life in Palestine at the time of Jesus, to assign acceptably accurate dates to the important events of his life, and to the periods immediately before and after it, and to suggest what influences and happenings made him what he was. Where the gospels and historians such as Josephus differ it would be wrong to assume without further evidence that Josephus is always right, the gospels always wrong: the one may just as well have used faulty sources as the other. But Josephus was a professional historian, the writers of the gospels were not; Josephus did not write to propagate a cause but to record what he believed were facts – the evangelists wrote to prove and to promote the truth of the beliefs they held. It has to be accepted that, from the few other sources of information available to us, what the gospels tell us about the circumstances of the life of Jesus suggests a somewhat uncertain local knowledge on the part of their authors; their sources were by no means as faultless as might be hoped, nor did they use their material as critically and as objectively as an unbiased historian would have done.

The gospels, with two minor exceptions, are concerned exclusively with events that occurred within the borders of Palestine, the country where Jesus was born, and in which he passed the one to three years of his mission – approximately the same area as that of the modern state of Israel. Except for the last few days of the period covered by the gospels, most of what they tell us took place in the northern province of Galilee, the area around the Sea of Galilee, also known as Lake Tiberias, and as far south as the strip of desert on the western side of the river Jordan, in Judea. Only rarely, until the end of his life, did Jesus actually go to Jerusalem.

The history of Palestine goes back some six thousand years, to when, around 4000BC it was occupied by the Canaanites. Some Hebrew (Jewish) people filtered into Palestine over the ensuing centuries. Shortly after 1300BC Moses led the main body of Jews (the Israelites) from Egypt into Palestine (though he himself never actually reached it); and, after struggles with the Canaanites and the Philistines to the north, their anointed king, David, was able to establish an independent kingdom in the area, with its capital at Jerusalem. After the death of Solomon, David's son and successor, the country split into two: Israel in the north and Judah in the south. Division weakened the Hebrew people, and Israel was defeated by Assyria (somewhat larger than modern Syria in extent) about 720BC, and over a century later, just after 600BC, Judah was conquered by the Babylonians under Nebuchadnezzar, who destroyed Jerusalem and took most of its inhabitants to Babylon in slavery. But the Babylonians were a broad-minded race, and the Jews were allowed to retain their religion and customs; and it was during their exile in Babylon that many of the books in the Old Testament were written.

In 539BC Cyrus of Persia defeated the Babylonians. Those of the Jews who had not already filtered back into the area were allowed to return to Judea in Palestine where, under a comparatively benevolent Persian rule, they were able to rebuild Jerusalem and re-establish a Jewish nation there.

Alexander the Great replaced Persia by Greece as the ruling power in 333BC, which in its turn was followed by Egypt, against which the Jews rebelled because Egypt was trying to impose a Hellenistic culture on them: and in 141BC they set up an independent state. This did not remain independent for long: the Romans, under Pompey, conquered Palestine and in 37BC put it under the kingship of Herod the Great, an Idumaean from the southernmost region of Palestine. Although not himself a Jew, Herod became "King of the Jews", and it was while he ruled the whole of Palestine, which included Galilee, Samaria, Judea, Idumaea and Perea, that Jesus was born. Herod the Great was capable and ambitious, and did much for Palestine, and rebuilt the Temple; dreaming of an independent Jewish kingdom; but he was cruel and unpleasant. Any report of a potential rival who might have thwarted his ambition to rule an independent Jewish nation would certainly have inspired the most violent jealousy, and Matthew's story (discussed in Chapter

VI) of the visit if the wise men and the consequent slaughter of the innocents and the flight of Joseph with Jesus and Mary into Egypt is entirely in keeping with his known character and behaviour.

When Herod died in 4BC the provinces over which he had ruled were divided up under his three sons, who were made ethnarchs or governors, a title slightly above that of an administrator or tetrach. One of these, Archelaus, was appointed ethnarch of Judea. He was an even more unpleasant man than his father. The Romans dismissed him in AD6, and he died in AD14. The provinces of Galilee and Peraea were governed by another son, Herod Antipas, who also took over Judea when his brother was dismissed, and it was he who was the "Herod" who was in Jerusalem at the time of the crucifixion of Jesus. He, in his turn, was banished in AD39 because he also wanted to be king. Such was not Rome's intention as it had already made clear when it appointed Pontius Pilate as Procurator of Judea in AD26. Palestine was then occupied by the Roman Army, the lower ranks of which were either mercenaries or conscripts from Syria (at that time another Roman province). In spite of this, ordinary people, except in some of the large cities, might well never see Roman soldiers, who were normally confined to such cities that had barracks for them.

The area covered by Palestine, although not extensive, is very varied in its topography. To the west lies the Mediterranean Sea, bordered by a coastal plain; this in turn is bordered by the mountains rising to some twelve hundred feet (400 metres). running from north to south, from Galilee, through Samaria to Judea; east of the mountains is a narrow strip of desert and the valley of the Jordan river. The river itself is well below sea level.

The most fertile regions are the northern part of the coastal plain and large areas of Galilee. In Galilee barley, wheat and rice, olives and grape vines, date palms, figs and pomegranates, were all among the crops Jesus must have known. The houses of ordinary people were usually built of baked mud bricks, still common in the Middle

East; only the houses of the wealthy and public buildings were of stone. Much of the agricultural land was owned by large landowners, on whose farms the villagers mainly depended for their livelihoods, working as hired labourers in conditions both primitive and difficult. The ox and the ass were the working animals commonly employed.

To the east of the Jordan lay the eastern plateau and in the extreme south the Negev desert, parts of Arabia, inhabited at the time of Jesus by the Nabataeans. To the north-east of Galilee lay the province of Gaulatini (after Herod's death ruled over by his son Philip), and beyond that the important Roman Province of Syria, with Damascus as its capital, then as now. Lastly, to the north of Galilee, and between it and the coast, was Phoenecia, with its two great ports, Tyre and Sidon, and its reputation for trade by sea throughout the Mediterranean and even as far as Britain.

The climate of Palestine is well suited to the kind of outdoor life that Jesus lived during his mission – rarely too hot or too cold. The summer can certainly be hot, but winds from the sea help to cool it. The winter is generally mild, but it can be cold, especially at night, and frost occurs in many parts during the three months from December to February. There is a moderate rainfall, but this is not sufficient to prevent life being lived largely out of doors.

In the northern provinces of Herod's kingdom the Jews were mainly Israelites, who were not considered "proper Jews" by those from Judea. And there were many who were not Jews, among them the Samaritans in Samaria, as the gospels clearly show. Ever since Alexander the Great had spread his Empire eastwards there had been a Greek influence in Palestine, and at the time of Jesus Hellenic culture was strong enough to penetrate and influence the thinking even of orthodox Jews. It was in Greek, in the "popular" Greek known as "Koine", that the gospels were written; it was in Greek that S.Paul wrote his epistles. It was Greek, not Hebrew or Latin, that was the language of the early Christian Church – and in modern western liturgies the *kyrie eleison* still lingers on to remind us of this fact. Although the Greeks had been reduced to a subject people and Rome had become the centre of the Empire, Greek culture was still held in high esteem: cultured Romans employed highly educated Greek slaves as tutors for their sons.

Jerusalem remained the capital of Judea, and the centre of the Jewish religion, with its great Temple and many synagogues (the places of worship of the Jews). The Temple was dominated by hereditary priests belonging to a sect known as the Sadducees, and the Temple priests were the traditional rulers of the Jews, and their position was taken for granted by them, at least by those of Judea. When Herod the Great was made king they had lost this traditional ruling power, but on his death it reverted to them, the ruling Roman authorities leaving the day to day running of Jerusalem in their hands. In fact, the Procurator, when he was appointed, was stationed at Caesarea, the Roman garrison town on the coast, some miles from Jerusalem, and he found it necessary to appear in the city in person only at times of festivals, when great crowds of pilgrims assembled, and disturbances might be expected. The Romans were very good at delegating power to those whom their subject populations were likely to obey. Thus the power of the Temple priests, and in particular of the High Priest, depended upon their remaining on friendly terms with their Roman overlords, which in practice meant kowtowing to them. Their policy was to submit to Roman domination so that the Temple, and the traditional worship of which it was the centre, might be preserved. The Sadducees are frequently mentioned in the gospels, not very favourably; they were undoubtedly jealous of their privileges and in the eyes of some of the Jews they were "collaborators" with the occupying Power: but if they were to preserve the Jewish religion and the central Temple worship they had little choice.

Although his family made its home in Galilee Jesus was undoubtedly an orthodox Jew, with his family and religion belonging to Judea. From what the gospels suggest, it appears that he accepted the Temple in Jerusalem as the centre of his own religion. As the first-born son of an orthodox Jewish family he was duly taken to the Temple when eight days old, where he was circumcised according to Jewish custom, and was thus enrolled a member of God's "Chosen People" – which is what the Jews believed they were. Again, when he was twelve, he was taken to the Temple, and possibly went through some religious ceremony similar to that of bar mitzvah, a ceremony that dates from about the third century but which may well have its origins in earlier practice. From that time he would have been accepted as a fully responsible "adult" as far as his religious life was concerned. Lastly, it was to fulfil his religious duties at the Passover that Jesus went to Jerusalem on the occasion when he was arrested and executed.

Not all the Jews were as ready to bow to the Romans as were the pragmatic Sadducees, and there were many who still believed that God would send a Messiah to deliver the Jews from the power of Rome and restore to it the supremacy of which they had dreamt for so long and the independence which they had so seldom enjoyed.

Besides the Sadducees, an important and influential group was that of the Pharisees. They were opposed to the Greek and Roman influences that affected the purity of their religion and were rigidly obedient to the Mosaic law. This led some of them to pay undue attention to rules and rituals – for example, with whom they should consort, what they should eat – rather than to ethical behaviour, but the best Pharisees were high-minded (some supported the teaching of Jesus), and they gave to Judaism much of its spiritual character.

A third group, of considerable importance, was that of the Essenes. Important though they were, they are not mentioned in the New Testament, neither in the gospels, nor in the Acts of the Apostles, nor in any of the letters of S.Paul or others. It is quite impossible that anyone living at the time in Palestine, anyone even only casually acquainted with life there, such as some of the Romans or Jews who normally lived elsewhere but occasionally visited Jerusalem, could have been ignorant of their existence. At first sight this omission seems to indicate that the Evangelists and S.Paul could not have known very much about Palestine in the days of Jesus. That they didn't, however, belies all belief. Paul was certainly a Palestinian born and bred; the writers of the gospels, whoever they were, certainly were either Palestinians or very familiar with the Palestine of the time. They could no more be ignorant of the existence of the Essenes than a normally educated Englishman can be ignorant of the existence of the Methodists. The obvious explanation for this omission is that the original Christians were recruited from the Essenes – that Christianity was, in its origin, an Essene evolution. If the gospels were written by and for members of the sect, they would have been the people for whom and about whom the gospels were written and their existence would have been taken for granted. Not only that – the name "Essene" was not what they called themselves but what others called them. In speaking of themselves they were satisfied simply with the usual "we" or "us"; and their belief, in the few places where it is mentioned, was known to them as "The Way of the Lord" (Acts,9,2), and members were just "believers". As far as the Essenes were concerned, it was the outsiders, the Pharisees, the Sadducees, the Samaritans, the Romans, the Egyptians, the Syrians, the Greeks who had to be named.

The importance of this cannot be stressed too strongly because it is the best reason for assuming that not only were his followers mainly Essenes, but that Jesus himself was an Essene, at least in upbringing and in his family. And if he was, much can be explained that otherwise remains inexplicable.

The Essenes were a devout sect of Jews whose relationship with other Jews may to some extent be compared with the Methodists as related to the Church of England – a reformist group rather than a breakaway one. They appear to have been divided into two groups or "orders": (i) those who lived strict lives in religious or monastic communities where life was ascetic and goods were shared, and (ii) those who lived in the community at large but to some extent apart from it, obedient to certain religious rules, rather like lay oblates attached to monasteries in the Catholic Church today. Cleanliness was important and they wore white garments – a fact, as will be seen later, that is important when interpreting certain events recorded in the gospels. Those not in monastic communities worked mainly as farmers and craftsmen – like the father of Jesus, who was a carpenter.

Where Jesus himself actually lived is not certain. He was almost certainly born in Bethlehem, in Judea, not far from Jerusalem. There is no reason to doubt the long unbroken tradition and the statements made by the gospels on this point. But where he had his home before and at the time of his mission is far from certain, beyond the fact that it was somewhere in Galilee. It was as a Galilean that he was known, and it was largely because he was so known that he was crucified, for Galileans were inclined to be considered subversive by their Roman masters, and several Galilean uprisings occurred during Jesus's lifetime.

Except for crossing the northern border to go to Tyre and Sidon (Matthew, 15,21; Mark,7,24), and his visits to Jerusalem, most of the events of Jesus's mission took place near the Sea of Galilee, in villages and open country. He seems to have avoided the larger towns. There may have been a good reason for this. He was a preacher who appealed to countryfolk and the ordinary Jew, not to the Hellenic-minded sophisticated townsmen. He used in his preaching parables that pictured the life of the fields and the farms, which those living in the villages would readily understand.

By tradition Jesus lived in Nazareth. Although Nazareth certainly existed by the time the gospels were written, it is uncertain whether it did during the lifetime of Jesus. If it did, it was still a very insignificant place. As mentioned in the notes in the Appendix, that Nazareth should have been named was probably due to a confusion of terms applied to Jesus. Jesus was known as a Nazarene; a Nazarene was a holy man, one who had taken a vow of celibacy. Its meaning, however, may have been unfamiliar to the editors of the gospel texts, who assumed it meant a person from Nazareth, which was known to be in the right area, and seemed to "fit". If Jesus did live in Nazareth it seems odd that the gospels never mentioned the important city of Sepphoris, only five miles away. There had been a revolt there in 4BC after Herod's death, the town had been laid waste by the governor of Syria and two thousand rebels were crucified. It was then rebuilt, and became an important town for the Romans. But at the very time Jesus was supposed to have been taken as a child to Nazareth the district must have been in some turmoil, and if Joseph was seeking somewhere safe to live Nazareth, so near to Sepphoris, was certainly not the district to choose. It may have been the destruction of Sepphoris that caused the growth of Nazareth, as a place to settle for the Jews who escaped the slaughter of Sepphoris, or for those unwilling to bow to the Roman rule there. By the time Jesus was a youth Sepphoris was again the most important city of the area. What appears more certain is that during the short period of his mission Jesus made his headquarters at Capernaum, and prior to his last visit to Jerusalem it was in the neighbourhood of Capernaum, by the shores of the Sea of Galilee, that most of the events recorded in the gospels seem to have taken place.

This was the country into which Jesus was born; this his background, his people, indeed, his world. To the ordinary Jew the possibility of an independent Jewish nation above all other nations was not too much to believe in. Most would have had only vague ideas of the extent of the Roman Empire which at the time included the western fringe of Asia Minor, the northern fringe of Africa, all Greece, Italy and Sicily, and much of the Iberian peninsular and

Gaul. Merchants and scholars would have had contact with Persia and India. But the peoples of China and the far east were largely ignored; the very existence of the Americas was unknown. The picture that the Jews had of God was a very human one. Although he was the only True God, the Creator of all things, he was credited with very un-godlike feelings towards the human race, caring only for the welfare and future supremacy of the Jews. The Essenes, who were against slavery as a violation of human rights, showed the beginnings of a belief in the universal brotherhood of all mankind, a belief that was certainly embraced by Jesus although, inevitably, he must have shared most of the ideas about the world current in the society in which he lived, inherited from the culture in which he was brought up.

Chapter III
Gospel Texts – Have Originals Survived?

The gospels tell us little or nothing about most of the life of Jesus. But they do claim to give us a reasonably complete insight into the mind and teaching of Jesus during his final mission, his arrest, trial and execution. They also cover a brief period after his crucifixion. Except for a few remarks by S.Paul, whose letters preceded the gospels, and a brief mention in a somewhat suspect passage in the writings of the Jewish historian Josephus, there is no other source of information about him from reliable near contemporary Jewish or Roman sources.

Before considering what the gospels do tell us it is essential to know whether the texts that we have are the originals – are they substantially what they claim to be?

It was not until the Third Council of Carthage in AD397 that it was agreed which gospels were to be included in the canon of the New Testament – that is, which were to be accepted as divinely inspired, which should be rejected as heretical. Only the four gospels attributed to SS.Matthew, Mark, Luke and John were included. A number of other gospels had appeared at various times and were in use in one or another area of Christendom. Some of these were in use up to the time of the Council, including the gospels of Barnabas and James and the Acts of Thomas. As a result of the Council most copies of these were destroyed, but a few did survive.

The four gospels selected, and which now form part of our present New Testament, were possibly as good a choice as could have been made at the time, although it is now generally accepted that the full authority of the authorship attributed to them is questionable. By the year 397 the texts had already been consolidated for a long time; in fact it seems probable that they took what was to be their final form early in the second century, around the year AD120.

Had many alterations been made in the texts after the time when copies were beginning to multiply there would have existed many very different versions of each of them by the fourth century. In actual fact, although there were a large number of minor differences, few variations of importance occur in copies or fragments of copies which survived from that period. These show that texts must have remained little altered for many years, going right back to the time when only very few copies existed. This means that already early in the second century the texts of all four gospels had become fixed; minor variations crept in from time to time, due mainly to human error in the tedious and demanding task of copying, often from old, damaged and probably, at times, from almost illegible copies; but for the most part such variations are insignificant. Had there been major differences disputes would have arisen as to who had the correct text: such disputes did not, however, occur.

It is from those very early definitive texts, written in Greek, that the gospels we have today have been translated into English. With every discovery of another ancient text or fragment it has become increasingly possible to work back to what must have been the original text, and the latest translations are thus nearer to the originals than earlier ones. But it must not be forgotten that they are translations, and subject to some extent to the interpretation of their translators.

It is unlikely that the Greek texts were direct translations from earlier Aramaic writings: if this were so it should be easy to translate them back into Aramaic – it appears that this is not so. But this does not preclude earlier Aramaic texts having been used as source material. For quotations from the Old Testament, however, the gospel writers did not translate from Hebrew texts, but used the Greek available in the Septuagint, the official Greek translation of the Jewish Scriptures in use at the time.

Whether there did exist earlier material in Aramaic – the everyday language of the Jews in Palestine – we do not know for certain since no such text, either original or copy, has survived: it is, however, reasonable to assume some such writings, intended for the first Aramaic-speaking Christians, did exist and were available to the authors of the gospels.

It is worth while remembering that, when analysing or interpreting the meaning of any given passage, too much importance must not be attached to the precise choice of words used by the gospel authors. The tendency of commentators to do so is a common error. The original authors were not necessarily scholars; Greek may not have been their mother tongue, and their vocabulary was probably limited. They may well have lacked understanding of the subtle differences between similar terms, and been less at home with the language than those who read them today. They would have given to the words they used the meaning that was current at the time in the area in which they lived, and would not have had the use of dictionaries, based on a wide range of writings, to help them choose a more appropriate word. Modern scholars may all too easily thus give to their words a meaning that was never intended, a subtlety never envisaged. It is unwise – but all too frequently attempted – to base a theory or a doctrine on a few words, even on the choice of a preposition, crediting the author with semantic or literary skills he probably did not possess. Perhaps it is the natural humility of the true scholar to assume in others an understanding of the language equal to his own: but in the case of the authors of the gospels their style suggests they were men of but modest linguistic ability.

The original copies of all the works of the great Greek and Latin writers of the centuries before and immediately after the time of Jesus have long since disappeared; and the original copies of the gospels, and of all the books and letters of the New Testament, have likewise perished. This is not surprising. For the most part they were written on papyrus. Clay and wax tablets, and also parchment, all of them more durable than papyrus, were known and used at the time. Wax and clay were clumsy, suitable only for notes and short records of such things as accounts; parchment was expensive, and at the time was little used – it only came into more general use for books several hundred years later.

Papyrus was both cheap and plentiful. It was made from strips taken from the pith of riverside reeds placed criss-cross and pressed together flat to form a sort of woven paper. Unfortunately it was not very durable; it was too flimsy to stand up to much handling, and it deteriorated in adverse climatic conditions, especially where the air tended to be damp. Some very old papyrus writings, stored in very dry conditions, often in jars, have survived for over two thousand years, though these tend to be brittle and flaky. The writings of the New Testament were not meant to be put away and stored, but to be widely and constantly used. The result is that they soon became too worn for use and had to be recopied. Texts containing parts of the gospels written on papyrus which have survived from the first two centuries of the Christian era are mostly fragmentary – and they are themselves parts of copies, not of originals. One of the oldest of these (some think the oldest) is a fragment of papyrus written on both sides in a style of handwriting used for Greek around AD150. It is today in the John Rylands Library in Manchester. Although it is small and contains only a few words, these correspond accurately with two fragments of the present text of John's gospel. As the two passages represented on the two sides occur close together this fragment is clearly from a codex – a document in book form, not a scroll. Although Jewish usage favoured scrolls, the introduction of texts arranged as books probably began in the first century A.D. Three fragments containing a few verses of Matthew (from chapter 26) in Magdalen College, Oxford, have recently been judged to be not later than AD70, and are also from a codex. Scholars do not agree on the actual date, but even if they are as early as mid-first century this is no proof that the whole text of Matthew as we now have it was already in existence at that time. A similar fragment almost certainly from a text in Mark (Mk 6,52-3) suggests that written source material, if not the final form of Mark, existed by that date (see *The Jesus Papyrus* in Bibliography).

There are some ten Greek papyri (as papyrus texts and fragments are called) dating from before the year AD300 with passages of sufficient length to be of value as confirmation of the accuracy of later complete copies. Obviously, there could have been differences in passages not covered by these fragments, but if two scraps of a copy of the text, taken haphazard from the whole, correspond with our present text it would suggest that some part, if not all, of our present text probably agrees with the text from which that very early copy was made, which in its turn could have been the original itself. Moreover, already in the early part of the second century – that is, shortly after the year AD100 – Christian writers were accustomed to quote extracts from the gospels. These works, like those of the New Testament, now only survive in later copies; and the quotations they contain could have been "edited" to agree with some later text known to the copyist. If a copyist found that a quotation differed from the text as he knew it he might have thought it right to "correct" it. But when the same quotation occurs in the work of different authors it is likely to be accurate and can then safely be used to control the gospel text from which it was taken.

Many modern English New Testament editions show where the major differences occur between the various ancient texts, and the Bible Society publishes Greek texts which give exhaustive details both of variations and of the different early manuscripts on which the text is based. The necessary information is thus available to everyone. Unfortunately most of us have to rely on others to translate the Greek into English, and such translations can never be completely satisfactory. The meaning of a Greek word or phrase may not be clear, it may be open to more than one interpretation, and translations will therefore differ. However careful the translator may be, however well versed in the two languages he is using, his own prejudices may be the deciding factor when he has to make a choice when deciding how to word a difficult phrase or thought. Moreover, our many different English translations of the gospels are always written in good English – in the kind of literary English current at the time the translation was made. In the course of time the meaning of the English words themselves may alter, and no longer mean to the reader what was intended by the translator. This will be enough to give the reader a false idea of what the original actually says. Our English translations have been written either by one individual or, more frequently, by one group working together, with the result that the style remains the same in all four gospels, and, indeed, throughout the whole Bible, giving the impression that it was all written in one same consistent elegant style. But this is very far from the truth. The Bible is a collection of many different books by many different writers who lived at different periods, centuries apart; some wrote in Hebrew, some in Greek. In the New Testament, as far as the gospels are concerned, there were probably at least forty years between the writing of their earliest passages and the composition of the final text of John: years during which ideas about Jesus underwent considerable changes, and which were inevitably reflected in the way in which he was presented to believers. It is all too easy to forget that the individual styles, and the grammatical errors and special vocabulary of each writer, are not reflected in the unvarying style of the elegant language of the English versions. Nor is it clear to the reader of any well phrased translation that the authors of the gospels were, in fact, writing in a language with which they were not all equally familiar, probably in some cases a second language, not their mother tongue.

When it came to reporting the actual words spoken by Jesus or by others, the authors had to translate the original spoken Aramaic into written Greek, thus to some extent being obliged to interpret the Aramaic meaning before deciding how best to put it. Such a

Greek translation of the Aramaic would most certainly be a much condensed version of what was actually said. After a further translation into English we have a translation of a translation – of Aramaic words spoken, remembered, orally transmitted before being written down – inevitably a shortened and possibly inaccurate paraphrase of the original spoken words. It is a pity, but as a fact of life it must never be forgotten that the elegant English of the Authorized version, a translation made over three hundred years ago, is not only already unlike the English of today, but even farther removed from the homely Aramaic used by Jesus. Though it may sound beautiful enough, it gives an entirely wrong impression of what it must have been like to have heard Jesus in person.

The "editing" of early texts, though it doubtless occurred, is not likely to have been serious enough to suggest that the texts that have come down to us have been significantly altered. Things could so easily have been much worse. We must be grateful to the early Church that when it became sufficiently organized to do so, it did its best to preserve intact the texts it believed authentic. Perhaps by as early as the year AD100, seventy or so years after the crucifixion, the three synoptic gospels had been copied and circulated sufficiently widely, and were well enough known by Christian writers and by those who heard them read in their worship, to prevent any later major alterations. They take us back not to Jesus himself but only to what the Church of the first quarter of the second century believed about him. What they reflected was what was believed about Jesus by those born too late to have known him or to have known those who had first-hand knowledge of him; their texts were based on information that had already been subjected to the influences of hearsay, misunderstanding, uncritical reporting by word of mouth – texts affected, on the one hand by the intrusion of a newly evolving theological philosophy and, on the other, by the absorption into the story of Jesus of elements of myth and legend. This does not necessarily mean that the gospels are worthless as historical records. But we are faced with the almost impossible task of deciding to what extent the gospels can be relied upon. This problem would be easier to answer if we knew for certain who wrote them, and when they were written: two problems that the next chapter will try to solve.

CHAPTER IV
THE GOSPELS: ORIGINS AND ACCURACY

"Gospel truth" has, in the past, commonly meant "completely true", a term arising from the long-held belief that the text of the Bible, and in particular of the gospels, was "the word of God", inspired by him, of unimpeachable truth. This belief is now no longer held by the majority of Christians, although there are some who still cling to it in the face of all evidence to the contrary. Even though we may agree that the texts themselves are virtually textually accurate, that is to say, that they have come down to us in what is something very close to the form they had finally acquired by the time they were generally accepted as part of the Scriptures by the early Church, unfortunately that was so long after the events they record that detailed historical accuracy cannot be expected. Textual integrity does not mean, regrettably, historical accuracy. This is quite another question. We may well have the texts: but how reliable are they as history? There still remains the all-important problem of trying to assess their historical truth. Did what they say happened really happen? Did Jesus really say what they tell us he said? Did he do what they say he did? Is what they tell us fact, or legend loosely based on fact, or pure invention?

The picture the gospels draw of Jesus inevitably became coloured by the doctrines current at the time they appeared in their final form. By that time the teaching of S.Paul was universally accepted; his letters (the "Epistles") had been written and widely circulated. Jesus and the disciples who had known him were all dead.

The gospels cover the brief period of Jesus's active ministry, usually believed to have been three years (but some say much less). During that time he was probably preaching almost daily. Inevitably, records as brief as the gospels could, at best, contain only a very small proportion of what he said during those few months of concentrated activity, whether in his public life or in private conversation and discussions.

Much of what the gospels do tell us can be no more than what lingered in the memories of his listeners and survived long enough to be written down a generation or so later: at best a brief resumé or digest of what he said rather than the actual words. As the apparent editor or copyist wrote at the end of John: "There are many other things that Jesus did. Were they all to be written down, one by one, I suppose that the whole world could not hold the books that would be written." (John 21,25). An exaggeration, perhaps: but the point made must not be overlooked.

Anyone who receives two different accounts of the same event as reported in the newspapers or on television knows how, within only a few hours of an event, reports of what was done or said may differ widely. It can hardly be expected that reports of what Jesus said were accurately remembered, word for word, even supposing the writer was himself present and had no special axe to grind.

It has been suggested that someone might have written down the words of Jesus immediately after he had been speaking – possibly S.Matthew. As a former tax collector he would not only have possessed the writing tools but also would have been accustomed to making notes. It is, however, unlikely. For the most part Jesus preached out of doors, and he and his followers, S.Matthew included, were constantly on the move. Making and keeping written notes would not have been practical – there were no fountain pens or even pencils, no convenient pads of paper on which notes could be jotted down – such a practice was both impracticable and unknown at the time. Moreover as far as his listeners were concerned Jesus was speaking for those present, not for posterity. That there would one day be a need for such a record could not have been foreseen. That S.Matthew might have made notes at a later date, probably after the crucifixion, is possible, and the existence at one time of such a work was mentioned by an early Christian writer. Matthew, as a former tax collector, was probably the best equipped of Jesus's followers to undertake such a task, and it might have come naturally to him.

The gospels frequently appear to give the actual words spoken by Jesus, but it is often impossible to make sure which are meant to be his own words, and which are the writer's comments on them since the Greek does not have quotation marks. Frequently there is no way to distinguish between the one and the other: reported speech or comment. The problem of separating the one from the other is especially noticeable in John, where comments are common.

The report of a discourse like the "Sermon on the Mount" (Mtt 5,3; Lk 6,20) contained teaching simple and striking enough to be recalled with some accuracy, but the different accounts of this passage as given by Matthew and Luke clearly illustrate the approximate nature of such recollections. It is, of course, probable that Jesus repeated the same sermon more than once, and not always in the same words, and what we have is a summary of many sermons. Moreover, it is easy to overlook the obvious fact, already mentioned – but important enough to repeat – that however accurately the words of Jesus were remembered the authors of the gospel texts had to translate the original spoken Aramaic into Greek. In so doing they were obliged to some extent to interpret the Aramaic meaning before deciding how best it should be put into Greek. Such a Greek translation of the Aramaic spoken by Jesus or by others would most certainly be a version, often a condensed version, the accuracy of which depended not only on a long-term memory but also upon the understanding and linguistic skill of the translator, which may not always have been fully equal to the task.

It is not possible to attribute to Jesus every word he is recorded as saying without involving him in contradictions and in ignorance of the world about him. But the fact that the future did not always unfold as he foretold, as recorded by those who had, by the time they wrote, the benefit of hindsight, suggests that in such cases as these he was probably accurately reported – the writers would have preferred to have been able to put into the mouth of Jesus more accurate prophecies.

It is essential in assessing the value of a document as historical evidence to establish, as nearly as possible, both the date it was written and the authority of its author and his sources. As far as the gospels are concerned, in spite of the efforts of countless scholars these are questions the answers to which have proved elusive.

The order of the first three gospels, as they appear in most versions of the New Testament, is Matthew, Mark and Luke. These three are known as the "Synoptic Gospels", so called because of the many similarities between them (from a Greek word meaning "seeing together"). Before these three gospels had arrived at something approaching the definitive form in which we now have them Christianity had begun to spread to those who had no personal knowledge of Jesus – those born after his crucifixion and those living too far away to have had any immediate contact with him or his close followers. Surviving eye-witnesses were dying, and the need had arisen to preserve in writing what hitherto had been available from recollections of the original companions of Jesus and other contemporary sources, and passed on by word of mouth – the "oral tradition". But even before then there would have developed some need for written records for groups of early Christians not in contact with those who had known Jesus or known those who had been authorized by him to pass on his teaching orally. As time went by the need would also have been felt for written accounts for reading to Christians when they gathered together for worship, and also for the instruction of those seeking baptism. Those who were Jews – and references to the Jewish Scriptures makes it clear that it was for Jews that the gospels were largely written – would have already been accustomed to hearing the Scriptures (until that time the books of the Old Testament) read at religious meetings to provide material for both preaching and instruction. It was thus entirely natural that when the followers of Jesus met together they should want to hear about what he had said and done, and some form of records written for this purpose may have been in existence from a very early date, perhaps as early as a year or so after the crucifixion, though there is no way of knowing how many were actually produced, nor how much they contained. It is probable they were brief and incomplete, a collection of "sayings" attributed to Jesus, or the story of one or two parables, depending on the limited sources available to whoever composed them – sources that were not always reliable. In the course of time the best of these would be exchanged, copied, compared and added to. Written on papyrus, individual copies would soon wear out, but some of them must have been available to the authors of all four gospels. These early notes did not survive: once their contents had been absorbed into one or more of the definitive gospels there would have been no need to preserve them by recopying as separate texts, and they would soon have disintegrated if they continued to be used.

That some such written material dating from before the composition of the existing gospels did indeed exist is obvious from similarities between the three synoptics. It has been assumed that there was a document, now lost, which has been named "Q" (from the German word *quelle*, meaning "source"), used by all three. In all probability there was more than one such source, and "Q" should more properly be considered a number of early writings, in Aramaic or in the more literary Hebrew, and in Greek. Of these, some were used by one or other of the gospel writers; others were shared by two or more of them. S.Luke, indeed, clearly states that "many have undertaken the task of writing an account ..." (Luke,1,1).

The date when the gospels were written is clearly of importance if their historical value is to be correctly assessed, the longer the gap between the event and the recording of it, the less accurate the record is likely to be. Unfortunately it is now impossible to establish for certain which parts of the gospels formed the original text, nor is it possible to establish with any degree of certainty the dates when those original texts were written. Attempts to do so have given rise to many different opinions. Those who fervently believe in their message are inclined to be influenced by arguments for their early composition, and usually disregard all but the most obvious cases of "editing"; those who wish to belittle Christian teaching are all too ready to accept arguments for their having been written too long after the events they record, and to have been subjected to so much revision, to be of any real value.

Opinions differ as to whether the synoptic writers knew about the destruction of Jerusalem in AD 70. Clearly, if they did they must have written after that date. The destruction of Jerusalem and the result of the revolt against the Romans appear to be referred to by a prophecy attributed to Jesus, given in some detail in all three synoptics (Mtt 24,1; Mk, 13,1; Lk 21,5), but none of them suggest that the prophecy had been fulfilled: on the contrary the events foretold are linked to the coming end of the world, not to a popular rising of the Jews against the Romans. Doubtless, when the fall of Jerusalem followed the Jewish rebellion many Christians took this as a sign that the promised end was indeed near – a belief which certainly did reign among early Christians for many years, only gradually losing importance as time passed and nothing happened. The prophetic description of what was to happen and what actually did happen are sufficiently different to suggest that they were written before AD 70. Certainly Jesus's prophecy that no stone of the Temple would remain upon another, as already noted, was inaccurate, and had the account been written after the event it might well have been worded to fit better the known facts. This is not a proof that the synoptic gospels were written before AD 70, but it is an argument in favour of that theory.

Biblical commentators are not agreed on the order in which the gospels were written, although most (but not quite all) accept the traditional view that the last was John. Most think that the first was Mark, but with some opting for Matthew. However, it seems reasonable to suppose that, as there are good grounds for putting either of them before the other, they were probably independently written, but shared some common sources, or used sources which in their turn were based on some yet earlier common source material. It is also certain that both gospels were added to and edited before the definitive text was established. It is also possible that each of the three synoptics was to some extent "corrected" by, or added to, by using material from one or both the others when they became available for comparison, to make them "agree". It would not have been considered wrong to make such additions to fill in what was considered incomplete, since the object of the gospels was to supply the fullest information available. Moreover, as the gospels were the "evidence" for what the church believed it was essential that they should support that belief and there can be little doubt that interpolations in the original texts were added to ensure they did so. There are some passages which could only have been written by those who were "wise after the event". In his thoughtful and erudite *"The Evolution of the Gospels"* (Yale University Press, 1994) J. Enoch Powell, who is a Greek scholar of exceptional ability, has shown how, and to some extent why, in his opinion, the gospel attributed to S.Matthew was built up with additions, and additions to additions. All four gospels were subjected to similar treatment.

Because the three synoptic gospels share material from earlier sources, the actual date of their final definitive form is not so important when assessing their historical value as the accuracy of their sources. Unfortunately, since those sources have all perished, we have nothing better to go on than reasoned guesswork. Some material used might have dated back to AD35-45, the period immediately following the crucifixion, when the words and deeds of Jesus were still fresh in the memory of his disciples. Like all such recollections they would have been limited, selective and distorted. Anyone coming away from an impressive sermon can only remember parts of it, those parts which happen to strike a sympathetic cord with the listener – different parts for different persons. Each of those who heard Jesus speak would have selected subconsciously those passages he most wanted to hear – or, in the case of those with an uneasy conscience, those passages he most feared. There would be incomplete understanding of the arguments, however simply put, and in the recall an ever-growing distortion of what was really said. The disciples themselves, no doubt, received constant and repeated instruction, but the written words of the gospels more probably record not their own memories but records of the memories they passed on to others. Thus it may be true to say that while the gospels reflect the tenor of Jesus's teaching, they rarely give his actual words.

The most likely passages that retain the closest approach to Jesus's own words are almost certainly the parables. Jesus doubtless used the same parable several times with different audiences, so that those who worked with him would have come to know them almost by heart. They are little gems of story-telling, easy to remember and to understand, too perfect in their construction and wording to be unduly distorted in their remembering. But even these show, by the variations in the versions of the same parable in different gospels, that the remembrance of them was only approximate. A good example is the parable of "The Sower", given by all three synoptics (Mtt 13,3; Mk 4,3; Lk 8,4). In the first two the story is almost, but not quite, the same, word for word; in Luke the wording differs more, although the story remains basically the same. Their sources may have been texts which originally emanated from memories of two different occasions when the same parable was used, since Luke gives the story in a context different from that of Matthew.

On the other hand events of a miraculous nature such as the frequent cures are much more likely to have been adorned in the course of retelling. It is human nature to exaggerate when describing some extraordinary event. After being repeated a couple of times the story loses something of its wonder in the mind of the teller, who feels it needs embellishing to retain its wonderment. Once one small miraculous event is believed yet greater wonders are looked for, and become easier to accept.

Where no eye-witnesses were available, as in the accounts of the temptation of Jesus, or where so much time had elapsed as to make it impossible to ascertain the facts, with perhaps only a few vague memories or the expected fulfilment of old prophecies to build upon, as in the birth stories, such meagre sources had to be filled in by the imagination of the writer to supply the details demanded by readers, stories consistent with that conception of Jesus which the writer wished to convey, and with the beliefs current at the time they were written or edited.

We thus have what is, in fact, a mixture of imagination, half-memories, subjective reconstructions of words and events, explanatory or doctrinal interpolations, and uncritical embellishments – sadly, very far from the "gospel truth" once generally accepted. When it is understood how varied were the ingredients that went into the composition of the gospels in their final and definitive form it is not surprising that they contain here and there otherwise inexplicable inconsistencies.

Although the three synoptic gospels are very similar in content, and although all four gospels cover the same period, and are concerned with the teaching, mission, trial and death of Jesus, they are nevertheless four different books, and each deserves individual consideration.

Matthew

About the year AD120, some fifty years after the gospel attributed to S.Matthew received its final form, the early Christian writer Papias (c.AD70-150.) wrote of a book attributed to the apostle Matthew entitled "The Oracles of The Lord", written in Hebrew, of which no trace remains. These "oracles" (*logia*) may have been lists of Old Testament prophecies fulfilled by Jesus, since the gospel attributed to S.Matthew has many examples which could well be based on such a list.

It has already been suggested that S.Matthew, having been a tax collector, would have been well equipped materially and by his early professional practice and later time spent in the company of Jesus to undertake a written record such as that mentioned by Papias. If it did contain many references to the Hebrew Scriptures this would indicate that the work was intended for use by Jews, and S.Matthew, in spite of his profession, was himself a Jew. This is clear from his name Levi, which he appears to have used at the time Jesus called him to be a follower. The name suggests he was of the tribe of Levi, which was a priestly tribe. Whether his name Matthew was given to him after his calling is not known, but it is also of Hebrew origin, meaning "Given by Jehovah". Perhaps he adopted it when he became a disciple. As an official working either directly or indirectly for the Roman authorities he would have been considered a collaborator by his Jewish neighbours. That Jesus should have selected a tax-collector as a disciple shows that he was not worried about the background of his followers – that he chose them for what he judged they were worth, regardless of public opinion. S.Matthew does not seem to have betrayed this confidence: he was still among the close disciples of Jesus when they gathered together after Jesus finally left them (Acts,1,12).

The present Greek text that bears the name of Matthew shows so many signs of having been altered and interpolated that it can no longer be called the original work of any one author. There are a number of parables in Matthew not given in the other gospels which presumably came from a source the others did not possess; it may well be these came from Matthew's supposed "Oracles" which formed the modest original material to which, in the course of time, more was added as a Greek text gradually came into being, the name of Matthew as author being retained to give authority to the final work. No writer of the early second century is known to have queried the authorship.

Although the "Oracles" may have provided the original basic material for this gospel it is the opinion of scholars with a knowledge of both Aramaic and Greek that Matthew is not a direct translation of an Aramaic text since the Greek does not lend itself easily to translation back into Aramaic.

The Greek Matthew which we now have, with its frequent references to, and quotations from, the Old Testament prophecies, clearly intended for converts from Greek-speaking traditional Jewish communities, doubtless enjoyed a wide distribution: such communities had been scattered around the area of the Eastern Mediterranean from before 500BC. They would have been familiar with Matthew's frequent quotations from the Old Testament, familiar with them in their Greek form from the Septuagint translation commonly used by Greek-speaking Jews.

Although opinions differ as to whether or not Matthew made use of Mark, or vice versa, it is more certain that Matthew did not make use of Luke. This is clear from the differences in the accounts each gives of the same events. Of these the most striking are the differences in the birth stories (dealt with in detail in Chapter VI). These two gospels also give different lists of Jesus's ancestors, Matthew (Mtt 1,1ff) working forward from Abraham to Joseph, the putative father of Jesus, and Luke starting with Joseph and working back to Adam (Lk 3,23) both making a point of including David and Abraham. The two lists vary considerably. Matthew's genealogy is clearly a later addition placed before the original beginning.

There are events, among which are the Flight into Egypt and Slaughter of the Innocents in Matthew (2,13 &16) and Jesus as a boy in the Temple, in Luke (2,22), which would surely have been included by both had the text of the one been available to the other.

There are other similar passages, parables, healings and teaching, some in Matthew, some in Luke, which the other would have been unlikely to have ignored if known. Such differences, combined with so much that agrees, suggests that both were written about the same time, each in a different area, addressed to different communities, the text of neither having had time to reach the area where the other was written, but both having used some shared sources. Where both Matthew and Luke have the same material this is often also shared with Mark, strengthening the theory that there were a number of sources available to all three, whilst each also had his own individual sources.

The very brief reference to the period following the crucifixion, (Mtt 23, 16-20) must have been added at a much later date as it contains the words "baptize them in the name of the Father, and of the Son, and of the Holy Ghost", which Jesus would certainly not have said: this is simply using part of the later liturgical language from the ritual of baptism, as used in the early Church at the beginning of the second century.

Mark

Mark is the shortest of the gospels. As in the case of Matthew, the earliest reference to it in early Christian literature occurs in the lost writings of Papias, quoted by later writers, notably by Eusebius (c.AD264-340), bishop of Caesarea. According to Papias, Mark was written by the S.Mark who was a companion of both the apostles Peter and Paul in the twenty years or so after AD35. If this is correct the writing would probably have been undertaken, after S.Mark finished his missionary work, at Alexandria, where he is believed to have finally settled. That S.Mark was the author of the gospel that bears his name seems to be indicated by a couple of incidents recorded in it which may be personal recollections, making him an eye-witness to some of what he records. One is the story of the young man whose garments were torn from him when he avoided arrest (Mk 14,52), something that seems unimportant in itself but which would have meant much to the young man concerned. The other incident is that of the appearance of a young man at the empty tomb, dressed in white. It must be remembered that white was the customary colour worn by Essenes, and Essenes would certainly have been numbered among the followers of Jesus (Mk, 16,5). If Mark, as an Essene, was both this young man and the author of the gospel in which the story appears, he may have had personal experience of other events of which he writes. The main body of the text, however, seems to be what S.Peter told him when they worked together. It is again Papias who confirms that S.Mark was for some time the companion and amanuensis (that is, secretary) of S.Peter. As such, he was probably better qualified than Peter to write Greek, although scholars do not consider that S.Mark was fully at home in the language. Papias also says that the gospel was, in fact, originally called "The Recollections of Peter". For the most part the text could well be based on the experiences and memories of Peter, who was present at so many of the events it records.

Some historians say S.Mark left Peter to go to Alexandria, and wrote his gospel there. Others think he wrote in Rome, after Peter's death there in AD67. There is no firm evidence that Peter went to Rome, but if he did, and if (as tradition has it) he was crucified there upside down, Rome, for a Christian Jew, was no safe place to be: the rebellion in Palestine had just broken out, and it is difficult to see how the secretary of someone just executed could peacefully remain there writing his recollections! Alexandria, however, was well away from both Rome and Jerusalem. It was a city famed for its literary culture. An authoritative life of Jesus for the Greek-speaking embryo Christian community, recruited from the Essene settlement there, was probably needed, and S.Mark would have been the obvious person to provide it. Clearly he must have written for some such purpose. Since there would have been no reason to write this gospel if Matthew was locally available, it is probable that at about the time Matthew was being written elsewhere, S.Mark produced his own composition, using copies of some material already available not only there where the final text of Matthew was being produced but also in Alexandria, to which he added further details from what Peter had told him or what he himself had witnessed. This would explain, among other problems, how he was able to give more background detail for material which he shared with Matthew, material for which Matthew did not have the benefit of S.Mark's own, or S.Peter's, personal recollections.

Owing to the special authority attached to the name of Matthew, and the general preference for that gospel as shown to it by the early Church, Mark may have undergone much less in the way of copying, and was for a while in danger of being lost. By the time it was given canonical status it had lost its original opening, with the result that the text we have starts somewhat abruptly. The first three verses of Chapter 1 seem to have been added later to replace what had been possibly a much longer beginning.

There are also several endings to Mark, presumably also replacements added to different copies made after the original ending had been lost. This would suggest considerable handling of the original work, or perhaps of a couple or so of early copies made from it in Alexandria, so that by the time further copies were required for wider distribution the original beginning portion and end were already missing. If the original Mark was written in codex form (with pages rather than on a scroll) such a loss is easy to understand.

The two verses near the end of Mark (Mk 16,12-13). which briefly tell of Jesus's appearing to two disciples while travelling, appear to refer to the two travellers to Emmaus whose story is more fully given by Luke (mentioned below) and hastily borrowed from his (by then well-known) story, to help replace some of the lost material of Mark's original ending.

Luke and Acts of the Apostles

It is quite possible that the gospel attributed to S.Luke was written by the Luke who was a companion of Paul on much of his travels. He was probably a Greek-educated Jew and a physician. He is believed to have been born in Antioch, and brought up in a society largely influenced by Greek culture, and some believe he was himself a Greek: but his familiarity with the Jewish Scriptures and tradition, and his apparent familiarity with Essene writings, make this improbable. He also wrote "The Acts of The Apostles", as a continuation of his gospel, to record the doings of the early Christians and the missionary journeys of SS.Peter and Paul – especially S.Paul. Both the books attributed to him are written in the same educated Koine Greek. The gospel is obviously addressed both to non-Jewish Christians, and to Jews who had, like Luke himself, a Greek education. As already suggested, like Matthew he used some of the "Q" material, besides other sources of his own. In fact he starts his gospel by explaining that "he too" had decided to do what "many others" had done – to arrange in narrative form what had been handed down by eye-witnesses and ministers of the word. This statement suggests there were, indeed, many early written records which have since been lost. He speaks of the things that had taken place in his own time, which would make him a contemporary of the apostles.

Unlike the authors of Mark and John and of such parts of Matthew as were eye-witness accounts, Luke seems to have had no personal experience of Jesus, but when travelling with S.Paul he would have had close contact with many who had. On the other hand, in the Acts he includes himself as having taken part in many of the events he records – using, when he does so, the pronoun "we". The Acts end somewhat abruptly some time before the execution of Paul in Rome in AD64, about which S.Luke appears to have known nothing. Nor does he say anything about S.Peter in Rome. It looks as if S.Luke must have left Rome some time before either of these events occurred (supposing Peter did go to Rome).

Where S.Luke finally went is not known, though early writers suggest he died of old age in Greece, and it may well have been that it was for some important personage in a Christian community there that he wrote. His gospel would have been written before Acts – therefore by AD63 at the latest.

It certainly looks as if S.Luke had some contact with the Essenes. The *Magnificat* (Lk 1, 46) which he puts into the mouth of Mary, the *Nunc dimittis*, which he puts into the mouth of Simeon (Lk 2,29), and the *Benedictus* (Lk 1,68), the hymn of Zacharias, besides reflecting passages in the Old Testament are also very similar to known Essene hymns, and may have been taken from some lost Essene texts. That he was a physician is borne out by his apparent familiarity with medical terms, and his knowledge might have been learnt from the Essene "therapeutae". Although these were originally Egyptian Essenes, their medical knowledge would have been known to, and practised by, their brethren elsewhere.

Legend, without any real foundation, tells us Luke was also an artist and a poet – he certainly seems to have allowed himself "poetic licence" in filling in the gaps of his story. He is said to have known Mary the mother of Jesus. Although this seems possible since Mary was, according to his own statement in Acts (1,14), still in Jerusalem with the disciples after Jesus's departure, it is nevertheless improbable that Mary supplied him with information; his ignorance about events following the birth of Jesus would seem to rule this out (as explained in the chapter on the birth stories). The story of the meeting with Jesus by two travellers on their way to Emmaus (Luke, 24,13) is thought by some to be a personal recollection, only one of the two being named – the other being S.Luke himself. The main weakness of the author of Luke as an historian lies in his apparent inability to assess the value of the many different sources he claims to have used. Where he was himself a witness of the events he records, as in much of Acts, his testimony must be taken seriously; but where he was using other material he seems to have been too ready to accept hearsay for history. The sending out of seventy-two missionaries (Lk, 10, 1-13) is an example. This is not mentioned in any of the other gospels, but, had it happened it would have been an important event, one demanding careful planning, considerable preparation and organization; it also seems out of keeping with the usual character of Jesus's own practice. Thirty-six towns and villages, all within walking distance, would have had to have been targeted to prepare each for the intended subsequent visit by Jesus himself. The requirements to carry out such an undertaking would have needed an organization of papal or Billy Graham proportions without any of their modern aids to help in the logistic problems that would have arisen: and there is no suggestion that the planned follow-up was ever attempted.

John

It is generally considered that this gospel was written considerably after the others. According to an early tradition, accepted by near-contemporary Christian writers, the author was the S.John who was the "beloved" disciple of Jesus, and later an apostle. If so, he was a young man at the time of Jesus's ministry, and, by the time the gospel was written had reached a ripe old age. Tradition, again, says that John the apostle died somewhere about the year AD100. Thus it would have been at the very end of his long life that this gospel was written, probably about AD98, at Ephesus, a town on the western coast of what is now Turkey in Asia. By that time the other three gospels were widely distributed; not only were the stories about the life of Jesus known, but Paul's teaching had become the accepted theology of the nascent Church.

It is, however, somewhat improbable that the disciple John, a

Galilean fisherman before he was called by Jesus, would have had the training to write this philosophical book. He may have been well educated, the son of the owner of fishing-boats and an employer of labour, not just a simple working-class man. He may, also, have been a man of considerable intellectual ability whose studies in later life enabled him to produce so profound a work. More probably there were those in his immediate entourage, products of a Greek education, to whom he turned, at the end of his life, dictating to them his recollections, discussing with them the nature and significance of Jesus, and leaving to them to produce what he would have regarded as his own testimony – in other words, what today we would classify as a "ghosted" work.

This gospel reflects the philosophical ideas about the nature of Jesus and the purpose of his mission which had already started to evolve by the beginning of the second century, and is much more in line with the theories of S.Paul than were the older synoptics. It is more a treatise for the initiated, learned Christian than a simple book about Jesus for the layman and convert. For this reason much of John's historical material is selective, chosen to illustrate the ideas it was intended to promote. There was no need to repeat all that the other gospels had already told, although in some cases there appears to have been a wish to make minor corrections to what they had written, from S.John's own personal memories. The history of the events immediately prior to the crucifixion differs from that given in the synoptics. There is no account of the Last Supper beyond the words "Jesus and the disciples were at supper" (John,13,2) but much about what was said and done after the meal, not mentioned by the synoptics. By the time this gospel was written the commemoration of the Last Supper had already become part of the Church's ritual, using earlier accounts of its institution in what became the prayer of consecration. There would have been no need to include what everybody knew by heart.

There are several passages which show that S.John was the

inspiration for, if not the actual writer of, events recorded: for example, where the text refers to him as "the disciple whom Jesus loved" – the same disciple, as it is made clear at the end of the book, as he who was responsible for the information it contains. But there are equally a number of passages which seem to have been added from elsewhere. The magnificent Prologue, formerly read in Catholic churches at the conclusion of every Mass in the Roman liturgy, has a deep philosophical character which must have been the work of someone with a Greek rather than a Jewish background and upbringing.

The miracle of the wedding at Cana, the first miracle of Jesus's mission, is more in the nature of the "works of wonder" to be found in later apocryphal "gospels" – it seems out of character with Jesus as elsewhere portrayed in this and the other gospels, and may have been added by someone who thought it would show the divine power of Jesus: unfortunately it tends, rather, to raise doubts. There are those who believe that it is not an account of something that actually happened but is a symbolic story, the "good wine" that comes last being the life of the Kingdom of God which Jesus came to initiate. The whole last chapter of John is a later addition, written in a style sufficiently different from the rest to be the work of some other writer. It may have been inserted to establish the authority of S.Peter at a time when S.Paul was becoming dominant; it may have been an unattached record of an event that occurred at some other time which somehow was attached to John on the false assumption that it came from John's recollections. Quite possibly it is the work of "John the Presbyter" whom Papias mentions, apparently a priest of his own city, Hieropolis. It is clearly out of place in its present position, and has always given rise to speculation about its real origin and authenticity. The original ending, "Jesus did many other mighty works ...etc" (Jn 20, 30,31) was allowed to remain, but a similar ending was then added to the addition: "There are many other things that Jesus did ..." (Jn 21, 25).

The gospel does not follow a normal narrative plan, and one gets the impression that it is a collection of separate passages. This strengthens the belief that it was written by someone near to S.John, someone who collected together the old man's recollections and written reminiscences. The final editor of the gospel suggests as much just before its conclusion, when he states: "He is the disciple who spoke of these things, who also wrote them down, and we know what he said was true" (Jn 21,24). The "we" was either an editorial "we" or referred to those who together collaborated in the production under S.John's tutelage and formed his immediate entourage.

It must, however, be noted that as an alternative, the "John" who gave his name to this gospel could have been some other John, including the presbyter mentioned above, someone about whom little was known other than his name, and credit for the gospel was therefore transferred to the one John in the area who was best known. Since there is no other evidence for this theory the traditional belief seems more probable.

Summary

The gospels were not intended for the use of future historians; they were not official records of the life of Jesus. Their authors certainly did not imagine that their work would be used for either purpose in the years to come. Nor do they claim (as claimed for them later) to have divine authority or to have been divinely inspired. We can neither attribute to them infallibility nor treat them as we would a work of modern biography or history. Christianity did not arise out of the gospels – Christianity already existed a generation or so before the first of them was written. They were intended to support what, at the time of their writing, had become the accepted beliefs about Jesus. They are a product of Christianity, of the form that Christianity had taken when they were written, and their earliest texts were probably added to or amended as the early Church changed and crystallized. This is especially true of John, which not only reflects how far the theology of the Church had evolved some sixty-five to seventy years after the crucifixion but also how deeply its way of thinking had been penetrated and moulded by Greek philosophy.

Apocryphal Texts

There were numerous other products of the Christianity current in the second century, known the "apocrypha" – those writings which, often after being in use in various areas for many years, were finally condemned as heretical. Many of these were so-called "gospels", and included the "Gospel of Barnabas", which was accepted in parts of the Church until AD325, when it was declared heretical and copies were ordered to be burnt. How many others there were that enjoyed the same fate is not known as many have vanished without trace, but most probably there were several hundred. The majority of these were written after the last of the apostles had died (that of Barnabas is a probable exception), although they may have contained stories about Jesus that were of earlier date. Some were mainly based on the existing canonical gospels, some were merely lists of sayings of Jesus, some purported to give new information about his life and childhood. Although they give useful information about the beliefs of some Christians at the time they were written, from AD125 right through until a couple of hundred years later, they do not add any worthwhile information about Jesus himself. Other apocryphal works of a similar nature included so-called "Epistles" and "Acts". Writers of the second and later centuries had no hesitation in attributing authorship to various apostles – SS.Peter, Barnabas, Thomas, Philip and James among them – to boost the authority of their own inventions. They were finally declared non-canonical – either because they were thought not to be written by the disciple whose authorship they claimed or because they did not agree with the current teaching of the Church. Most were destroyed, severe penalties could be incurred by continuing to use them. Nevertheless some fragments, and a few fuller copies of the more important, did survive – the Gospel and the Epistle of Barnabas, the Gospel and Acts of Thomas being among them. The people of those days were no less intelligent than those of today, but being less well informed about the material laws of physics they found no difficulty in believing stories of supernatural events – the virgin birth, miracles, angels, for example – which fitted well enough into their own concept of what was probable: ideas which many modern minds, moulded in a more materialistic age, find improbable if not completely incredible. There can be no doubt that the miraculous element that pervades the gospel stories, and the accounts of Jesus's birth and resurrection, present intellectual difficulties. But how far are they essential elements in the story of Jesus? Are they frills which obscure the real Jesus?

Miracles have played so great a part in the history of Christianity, not only in the life of Jesus but in the lives of his followers throughout the centuries, down to the present day, that the subject requires consideration in a chapter to itself.

Chapter V
The Gospel Miracles

We have seen that the gospel texts which have come down to us went through a considerable amount of editing and "improvement" before they took on the definitive form they now have. Much that they contain must have been based on accounts passed on by word of mouth. Stories thus handed down orally invariably grow with telling, and notable events become marvels and then miracles.

Doubtless, many of the miracles attributed to Jesus can be explained in this way. That he was a healer of repute there can be no reasonable doubt, and his skills may have far exceeded those of lesser men of his day. As his reputation grew and was noised abroad, exaggerated stories would inevitably evolve, and, helped by the credibility of the uninformed people of his day, stories of miracles were easily accepted.

Nevertheless, many of the cures described in the gospels could well have taken place much as described: a cure can appear miraculous if effected by means unknown to observers, or if the illness cured is not all that it appears to be. That the human mind has power over matter, and that there are those who are able to employ this power, is a fact – a fact that was known to Buddhists for centuries before the time of Jesus. Much of their knowledge was doubtless passed on to the Essenes of Egypt when their missionaries reached there about 300BC, and this knowledge would in turn have been passed on to the Essenes elsewhere. Doubtless it was known to those who (as suggested in the next chapter) looked after Joseph and his family during the flight into Egypt, and those under whose guidance Jesus studied during his years of preparation for his life's main mission. There were certainly plenty of opportunities for Jesus to acquire any knowledge and skills already available to, and practised by, the Essene theraputae and their disciples.

It is also an indisputable fact that many illnesses, including those apparently entirely physical in nature, owe their origin to the sufferer's state of mind. Certainly, some of the cures Jesus is said to have effected could be attributed not to any miraculous power but to his superior knowledge and understanding of the way the human mind can affect the body – knowledge that had long before his own time been part of oriental culture, and still is.

Most of the miracles in the gospels – but by no means all of them – are concerned with cures: the blind made to see, the lame to walk. Some involved the "casting out of demons". Not knowing the real cause of such ailments as epilepsy and other inexplicable disabilities, being "possessed by demons" was the only way people of that time could explain why such infirmities occurred, so it was equally natural that if someone was cured of such an affliction the cure would be described as the "casting out of demons". It was a manner of speaking, just as our speaking of the sun "going down below the horizon" is a manner of speaking – something that, in its origin, was believed to be literally exact and which now, with the progress of knowledge, survives as an accepted metaphrase. The event can be true enough even if the way it is pictured and described is somewhat primitive!

Although not performed for self-glory, the miracles of Jesus, besides the good they did to those who were cured, were undoubtedly included in the gospels, as he appears to have employed them in his life, to enhance his authority as a teacher. They were "signs": and it is as "signs", not as miracles, that the Greek of the gospels terms them.

Strictly speaking, the term "miracle" is only correctly used when it refers to some event that is beyond explanation and seemingly outside the normal process of cause and effect. In practice, in everyday language, we frequently use the word "miracle" to describe some unexpected or chance occurrence which is not a miracle at all. For example, we might say of someone notoriously bad at settling his debts: "He actually repaid the £100 I lent him on the date agreed – it was a miracle." It might have been unexpected; but in the strict meaning of the term this was not a miracle. Some manufacturers of drugs or patent medicines advertise "miracle cures", and people speak of a "miraculous escape" when an accident is avoided by some lucky coincidence. None of these are real miracles: the results described as miraculous are all the normal outcome of perfectly natural causes. There is a sequence of cause and effect that is wholly in accordance with the known laws of physics.

In all probability, not all the "miraculous" cures which are related in the gospels and which actually took place much as described were miracles in the strict sense, although through the ignorance of those who observed them they appeared to be. What we do not know is to what extent these "miracles" actually did occur, and to what extent they are later inventions inserted into the story of Jesus to emphasize the divine character the gospel authors wished to attribute to him. "Signs and wonders" were expected of someone acting in the name or with the power of God – this was so much taken for granted that if none had existed they would have had to be invented. That the miracles of Jesus were not inventions but, though doubtless to some extent exaggerated, occurred in something like the manner and circumstances related, is suggested by their comparatively modest character. The events as described are, for the most part, both credible and in keeping with the character of Jesus. An example of the kind of miracle that is clearly fabricated is given in the apocryphal gospel attributed to S.Thomas. Jesus, we are there told, was five years old and playing by a stream (the muddy waters of which he commanded to be made clean) and he made twelve clay sparrows. Rebuked for doing this on the Sabbath, Jesus, instead of answering his father who asked him why he did so, clapped his hands and told the clay sparrows to fly away – and they came to life and flew away chirping. On another occasion when a playmate swept away with a willow branch water which Jesus had collected, Jesus, calling him a dunderhead, caused him to wither up like a dying tree. Such "miracles" are not difficult to recognize as fabrications!

Whatever may be the truth with regard to individual cures recorded, Jesus certainly had the reputation of being a holy man endowed with remarkable powers which, the gospels make quite clear, he invariably used for the relief of suffering in others, never out of such childish spite as in the apocryphal stories, nor for self-glorification – which is something that cannot be said of all those recorded as having enjoyed comparable gifts.

There are many disabilities of the body which have their origin in the mind, caused perhaps by shock or mental stress. Sufferers from angina know this all too well: an attack may come not from any undue physical effort but purely through anxiety or mental frustration. It may be "all in the mind", but the result is painfully physical. In the first World War (1914-1918) the present writer's uncle, a doctor in the R.A.M.C., had a patient who had been struck dumb by shell-shock. There were no tape recorders in those days, but it was possible to make a simple sound recording by placing a clean wax disc on a wind-up gramophone and talking into the trumpet. The doctor first had his patient hypnotized, and when he was in a state of trance carried on with him a conversation which he recorded in this way. When the "dumb" soldier came out of his trance the record of his conversation was played back to him. Astonished, he exclaimed: "But I can't speak!" A shock had made him dumb; a second shock cured him – by no means an unknown sequence of events in medical history. In the distant past, to those who observed Jesus at work, when he used such techniques as this, the resulting cures would have been accounted miracles. Yet miraculous they were not, though they were evidence of a superior understanding of the laws of nature.

Many of the miracles of Jesus may fit into this category; others may appear not to do so, but this may be due to our present limited knowledge. The truth may be that when we declare something to be contrary to or outside the laws of nature, we are in reality acknowledging that we are faced with something that goes beyond our knowledge of those laws – something that we cannot explain in terms of our present knowledge: something that has the appearance of being "impossible" as far as the known laws of science and physics are concerned – the known laws, not the laws in all their fullness.

It was not really very surprising, once Jesus had become recognized as a healer, that he should rapidly acquire, through hearsay, the reputation of a wonder-worker, and that even quite ordinary everyday events would have been turned into miracles. Thus the first miracle he is said to have performed, the changing of water into wine (John 2, 1-12), may have been no more than a somewhat distorted account of his having in some way helped out his host with wine from some unexpected source; and, on a later occasion, the inexplicable multiplication of a few loaves and fishes into sufficient food to feed thousands (Mtt 14,13. Mk 6,30, Lk 9,10, Jn 6,1) may have been the result of those who, hiding for themselves the food they had with them, when shown a boy giving away the little he had, were shamed into doing likewise. This story is told by all four gospels, and Matthew and Mark have a second similar one (Mtt15,22, Mk 8,1) which makes it seem that Jesus used this procedure often enough to have impressed the memory of it on many of the crowds he addressed. The story of the wedding, however, is told only in John, the gospel in which the divinity of Jesus is most strongly stressed, and may have been edited into the text for theological reasons without any foundation in fact.

In the course of Christian history, over the last two thousand years or so, there have been thousands of recorded cases of miracles. Some are doubtless pious inventions, some may have been cleverly contrived frauds to gain credibility or donations from simple-minded people, and others, based on fact, may have gradually grown more and more wonderful in the telling, like "the fish that got away" in an angler's tale. Human beings have a remarkable ability – even, it sometimes seems, a need – to believe in supernatural or inexplicable phenomena. Stories of the "Bermuda Triangle", so-called "photographs" of UFO's, mysterious circles in the fields of Wiltshire, even when shown to be fakes are still believed, some minds more easily convinced by the fake than by the disclosure of the truth. If in these sophisticated days such reactions persist it is hardly remarkable that in an age when the possibility of miracles was generally accepted, and their performance by someone reputed to be a "holy man" was taken for granted, their happening should have been readily accepted as part of the story of Jesus and his apostles.

In the Roman Catholic Church, the largest Christian organization throughout the world, the possibility of miracles happening is accepted. Apart from other rare miraculous events which are not cures, those that are claimed as miraculous cures are subjected to the most vigorous controls before their assumed "miraculous" nature is recognized. A decision, one way or the other, will only be reached if all the facts are known and fully investigated. The rules laid down are stringent. These rules cannot, of course, be applied to cures that are recorded as having happened in the past; such events have to be accepted at their face value. Their credibility will depend on probability, and on comparisons with the tried and tested cures of the present day. The most thorough organization for testing miracle cures is connected with Lourdes, in the South of France, where there is a well-known shrine, and to which pilgrims in their millions go constantly throughout the year, as they have done since the first cures were claimed there in 1858. There are many other places to which people go for "miracle" cures, and such cures have been claimed by people of many other religions; but if we want to examine whether they really do happen those claimed at Lourdes provide us with the best possible material for an investigation because nowhere else is there so strict a control, so thorough an examination into all the relevant facts, so strong a disinclination to accept as miraculous even the most remarkable cures. Indeed, so rigid is the control that in spite of the many thousands of improvements in health and apparent cures that have taken place at Lourdes over considerably more than a century, less than seventy have actually been recognized officially as miracles – approximately just five every ten years. At Lourdes, to be registered as miraculous a cure must first offer indisputable medical evidence that the person concerned actually suffered from the ailment for which a cure is claimed. It must, moreover, be something that, medically speaking, is considered to be incurable; it must be of a serious nature or potentially fatal and of an organic character proved by X-ray or other tests. The cure, when it occurs, must be complete (except for some scars or other residual reminders of it), and not requiring convalescence. A decision is not reached until re-examination of the patient some years after the event proves it is permanent.

To control these points, and any others that in individual cases may seem necessary, there is at Lourdes the internationally famous Medical Bureau, manned by fully qualified doctors, not all of whom are necessarily believing Christians. It is the task of this Bureau to examine the patient's medical history to make sure the ailment existed in the first place, then to make sure the cure took place without any effective medical treatment, and that no medical treatment was possible, and that the cure was medically inexplicable; and, finally, to undertake the examination several years later to ensure that it is permanent. There is also an International Medical Committee consisting of 30 doctors which meets once a year in Paris, and which confirms or rejects the inexplicable nature of the cures reported by the Medical Bureau. The conditions are so stringent that many cures are never tested, although the sufferers may be personally convinced their cures have been miraculous, and this conviction may be shared by their friends and acquaintances.

Some who seem to have been cured may not have had the necessary proof that their ailment was real or incurable, without which no investigation can be started; some may be cured some time after leaving Lourdes and not wish to return for examination.

The rare cures which are accepted as miracles are so accepted because they are beyond explanation by the laws of science or medicine as far as at present known. This means that such cures – those of the gospels or those of today – were or are inexplicable by the knowledge available at the time, but this does not mean that they were or are contrary to laws yet undiscovered. Those who witnessed the work of Jesus were simple folk living in an age when the total sum of mankind's scientific knowledge was very limited; and even today, with all our present knowledge, who shall say how much remains unknown? In spite of the rapid development of science during the last two centuries we may still be almost as ignorant as was Roger Bacon, who in the latter half of the thirteenth century claimed to know all that there was to know. Bacon thought he did; we know he didn't. While the very existence of what is unknown to science remains unsuspected by us we are inclined to assume that in this advanced age the "experts" are omniscient – although the experts themselves are all too well aware that they are not. If, as seems likely, Jesus had acquired much of the wisdom of the East, he would have had an insight into aspects of truth which modern materialism prevents the Western mind from grasping. His very ignorance of the modern laws of physics may have left his mind free to absorb the truths that such laws obscure. He certainly appears to have understood, better than most, the relationship between Mind and Matter.

There is one common element in all "miraculous" cures – those of the gospel and those of modern times – the element of faith – that is, of a state of mental conviction. It is apparent, however, that this "faith" does not necessarily have to be possessed by the person whom the miracle most directly affects. It seems that for a "miraculous" cure to occur there must be a sufficiently strong assumption "in the air" that it is possible. At Lourdes there are thousands of people gathered together; among them some who fervently believe in miracles. The force which they create appears to affect others who visit the place: some are too ill, or perhaps too unbelieving, to have the necessary mental attitude themselves. In the Middle Ages, the "Ages of Faith", when people more readily believed in miracles than they do today, that force would have been much stronger, less blocked by our modern materialistic view of things, and miracles resulted simply because they were expected. In the remote mountains of northern India a belief in the power of mind over matter which existed in the days of Jesus still remains strong today: materialism has not gained there the mastery that it has in our western world, and the power of mind over matter is still taken for granted. We of western civilization know that such things "can't happen", so they don't – we are much too preoccupied with the mundane matters, alas, to probe into the depths of man's greatest treasure – the human mind; but among those who believe they can happen, they do.

The miracles of Jesus were included in the gospels as proofs of his divine authority; the miracles which his disciples are recorded to have performed were offered as proof of the authority they had received from Jesus. It is ironic that the same miracles have become today, in the minds of many, grounds for disbelief! It is prudent to show a certain degree of scepticism: intellectual integrity demands it. But a healthy scepticism does not require the slamming of every door, and the blank refusal to enquire.

As it was expected, in Jesus's days, that anyone with a mission from God would be a miracle worker, it is not surprising that there were then, as there have been throughout history, charlatans who were skilful enough in the arts of deception to win for themselves unwarranted "divine" authority. There is, however, nothing in the recorded character of Jesus, or in the kind of miracles he is reputed to have worked, to suggest that he was himself in any way a charlatan. Nor were they charlatans who recorded the "signs and wonders": they doubtless accepted in good faith, and easily believed. They were, perhaps, too ready to accept what they heard, too uncritical in what they decided they ought to record, and were disposed to assume a miracle where perhaps no miracle existed.

For example, there is the story of the cure of the son of the government official, who came to Jesus, imploring him to go to his dying son. Jesus told him his son would live; the son did live, and a miracle was assumed. Yet it is quite reasonable to suppose that Jesus, on questioning the man, knew what was the matter with the boy and realized that his father's anxiety was without cause – a matter of experienced diagnosis which proved correct (John, 4,46ff).

It is noticeable that some of the miracles related in Acts as having been performed by the apostles were more improbable, and some of them less altruistic, than those of Jesus (e.g: Acts 5:5, 12 and 18). The Acts were written by S.Luke. Where he writes of his own experience his testimony is valuable; but where he reports from other sources he seems to have been unable to assess critically the reliability of his sources. Here, too, there are possible explanations for the "miracles" that he records. For example, when S.Peter cured the lame beggar it may be that what he actually did was to change the beggar's attitude, so that he ceased to want to beg – abandoning his pretence at being lame. (Acts, 3, 1ff). Professional beggars frequently adopt such methods – they do today, doubtless they always have done!

The gospels, in their portrayal of Jesus, found it necessary to make much of miracles because their writers wished to emphasize the belief that had by then evolved from the teaching of S.Paul, that Jesus was divine – a doctrine that was later to be more clearly defined in the various declarations of the early church Councils in the doctrine of the Trinity. But in reality, as an historical figure, it is not for miracles in the distant past but for his enduring philosophy that Jesus remains pre-eminent to this day.

Chapter VI
The Nativity – Early Years, and Mission

Once the divinity of Jesus was invented by S.Paul. it became necessary to devise a suitable origin for him, consistent with the ideas current at that time – ideas much influenced by both philosophy and by Greek mythology. Both Matthew and Luke recognized this need, and supplied it: each has a story to show that Jesus was no ordinary man. In the original beginning of Mark there may also have been some birth story – if there was there is now no trace of it. In the preface to the gospel of John that origin is described in the language of Greek philosophy. It must be assumed – there seems no other explanation – that when John was written, about the year AD98, although both Matthew and Luke must have been in circulation the birth stories had not been added. But those stories must have come from somewhere – they must have been believed by those who included them in the gospels: it is inconceivable that they were deliberate inventions. They are today so well known, so widely accepted, that they deserve special attention.

Even if the evangelists S.Matthew and S.Luke were responsible for their accounts of the birth and early life of Jesus as given in the gospels that bear their names, they would have had to rely on the memories of very elderly people, and on stories passed on by word of mouth, for what happened at an event that occurred probably before they were born, or, at best, when they were still small infants.

Some seventy years at least passed between the time of the birth of Jesus and the insertion into Matthew and Luke of the stories of it. These stories were meant to promote the by then current concept of Jesus as God Incarnate, the doctrine (as already mentioned) invented by S.Paul, and which had evolved during the period between the date of the crucifixion in AD33 and the composition of the gospels over thirty years later. Seventy years is a conservative figure, which takes us only to AD68, about the time the synoptic gospels were being compiled. But if it is correct that the birth stories were later additions, unknown to John in AD98, we must add another twenty years – not much less than a century between the event and the story of it. Even if these stories in their original form had been circulating soon after the crucifixion, a considerable period must have elapsed before they received their final form.

Matthew and Luke have different birth stories, each intended to portray Jesus as its author wished him to be perceived. Matthew, addressed mainly to convert Jews, concentrated on the fulfilment of Old Testament promises of the coming Messiah, Luke on the god-man idea which readers educated in the current Hellenic culture would find echoed in Greek mythology. Memories of Alexander the Great, who regarded himself and was regarded by the Greeks as a god, still lingered in the culture of those early Christians who lived in the very lands that Alexander had ruled three centuries earlier. The idea of a god-man Saviour was thus not without precedent, and found ready acceptance.

The two birth stories are longer than most passages that occur in one gospel only; and each differs considerably from the other. Of all the events in the life of Jesus recorded in the gospels none are so well known as these two stories. Because the birth of Jesus, usually called the Nativity, is celebrated at Christmas, now a major popular holiday, the stories are familiar to almost everyone wherever Christmas is celebrated, whether they are Christians or not. With carols on radio and television, cribs displayed in churches and shop-windows, and the nativity plays proudly produced in many primary schools throughout the United Kingdom, few in this country can escape knowing something of the story of the Child born in a stable, in the depth of winter, under the light of a great bright star, worshipped by angels and shepherds and the ox and the ass, and by the three kings from afar who came bringing gifts.

In other countries with a long Christian history, the situation is similar; in some it is inexorably mixed up with Santa Claus and his reindeer, bearing gifts from the North Pole, together with S.Nicholas or Good King Wenceslaus, turkeys, holly, Christmas trees and Christmas cards, and age-old local traditions many inherited from ancient pagan celebrations of the winter solstice and in more recent times popularized by Charles Dickens.

If we leave aside the pagan elements, the early introduction of the three Kings and the ox and the ass in the stable, together with the modern Dickensian and Victorian wrappings of Christmastide, and look at the accounts of the birth of Jesus as given in the gospels, to what extent can we accept them as historically reliable?

Although these two accounts differ in some quite important details, they can be fused into one coherent story. According to Matthew, Mary, the Mother of Jesus, a Jewish maiden, was found to be pregnant by her future husband, Joseph. He wanted to break off the engagement, but an angel – a messenger from God – told him in a dream that the Child which Mary was carrying had been conceived through the direct intervention of God. The Child was destined to save his people from their sins, and was to be called Jesus. As a result of this assurance, Joseph took Mary home as his wife, and in due course the Child was born in Bethlehem, a small town in Judea, a little over five miles south of Jerusalem. It was in Bethlehem that David was crowned king, and where he lived, and Jesus was a descendant of David through his father, Joseph. The story continues to tell how some learned men (not kings as in the well-known carol) arrived in Jerusalem from the East. The Greek word used, *magoi*, actually means an "interpreter of dreams" and also a "wizard" or "sorcerer", but it may have been the nearest word the writer knew to describe learned men who were probably astrologers. They said that they had seen in the stars that a King had been born to the Jews, and they had come to pay homage. At the time Herod the Great was the nominal king of the Jews in Palestine, and, alarmed by this news (as were other dignitaries in

Jerusalem, fearing for their positions), he asked the Chief Priests where it was that the prophets had foretold that the Messiah (or Christ – the awaited God-appointed King of the Jews) was to be born, and they told him: Bethlehem. So Herod, pretending he would want to go and pay homage also, asked the wise men to find the whereabouts of the Child and come back and tell him. They set out in obedience to Herod's request, and the star they had seen led them on until it "stood" over the place where the Child was. They went into the house, found the Child with his Mother, worshipped him, and gave him gifts of gold, frankincense and myrrh (aromatic resins). It was these three gifts which suggested to an early commentator that there were perhaps three wise men, though their number is not given by Matthew. Having been warned in a dream not to go back to Herod, they went another way home. Herod then ordered that all boys of the age of two years or less in the area of Bethlehem should be slaughtered to make sure this new claimant to be "King of the Jews" (the title granted to Herod by Rome) should not survive to threaten him. But Joseph, once more in a dream, was warned to flee into Egypt, and to stay there until he received news of the death of Herod. This he did, and when he heard that Herod was dead he returned to Palestine. Learning that Herod's obnoxious son Archelaus ruled in Judea (something the messenger seems to have failed to tell him), and advised by another dream, Joseph went on some 60 miles farther north to Nazareth in Galilee, where he made his home. This is the story according to Matthew.

Galilee was the northern province of Palestine, and since the death of Herod the Great it had been governed (under the Romans) by another of his sons, Herod Antipas, whom Matthew does not mention.

The story of the wise men has evolved in the course of time; and in many of the carols, and the many paintings of the Nativity, they have become three Kings (a very early tradition), and the ox and the ass have also been included (another early addition) – a good example of how stories – especially attractive stories – evolve. That some truth lies behind the story as given by Matthew is suggested by astronomic records – one of the few reliable ways of penetrating into the past. In 1603 Johannes Kepler, a German astronomer, calculated that in the year 7BC the two planets, Saturn and Jupiter, would have been in conjunction – that is, they appeared close together in the same area of the sky – and might have appeared as the bright new star of the gospel story. Kepler's calculation has since been confirmed by modern astronomers. Both astronomy and astrology were taken very seriously in Biblical days by those who studied the stars, and, although it is necessarily speculation, it is quite possible that certain learned men who believed in the telling of the future by the stars, and who lived in the East – most probably Babylon – observed this conjunction among the group of stars known as the constellation of Pisces, which was for them the sign of the West – the Mediterranean area including Palestine. For the Jews, Pisces was the star of Israel and the Messiah, and this would have been known in Babylon at least since the days when the Jews had been exiled there some five to six hundred years earlier. Indeed, it is probable that the "Wise Men" were themselves Diaspora Jews living in Babylon, as this would explain the importance they attached to their reading of the stars and their desire to undertake the arduous journey to Jerusalem. Further, Jupiter signified royalty and good fortune – the birth, therefore, of a king; and combining Saturn, Jupiter and Pisces, this king could surely be none other than that very King whom, as they well knew, Jewish tradition awaited to restore their freedom. And Saturn was, for the Jews, the sign of Protection – hence not only was he the King but also the Messiah. Having worked this out, these astronomer-astrologers set off westwards to find this King-Messiah.

    The journey might have taken many months. The travellers could have gone due West, across the stony desert that lay between the river Euphrates and Palestine; or they could have followed the easier trade route north along the Euphrates until they reached Edessa or thereabouts, where they would have turned west towards Damascus, and then south to Palestine by the normal trade route. Although the conjunction of the stars which initiated their journey took place in 7BC they would have waited for a suitable trading caravan before leaving, and considerable preparation would have had to be made for so long a journey. Over two years may have elapsed by the time they finally arrived in Palestine, and seen there the comet which Chinese records say appeared in the spring of 5BC. This they would have taken as a sign that they had arrived near their destination. It would have been natural to enquire at the palace of King Herod, since it was a king they sought. When directed on to Bethlehem, the gospel story says the Star "stood over" the place where Jesus was; but clearly this could not happen. A star may appear to be over a certain spot when viewed from one position; but if the same star is viewed from somewhere else at the same time it appears to be over some other spot: and an hour or two later it will have moved across the sky and appear to be over some place elsewhere.

Nevertheless, it is quite possible that their belief was confirmed on arrival at their destination by the appearance of the comet.

The date of the conjunction of the two planets does not give us the date of Jesus's birth since, even if it happened as suggested, all that we can say is that the Wise Men set off in or soon after 7BC. and finally arrived in 5BC. If Jesus was born when the "star" was first seen he would have been some two years old when they found him; and this would explain why Herod ordered all children under three years old to be killed, taking us back to 7BC for his birth, which agrees within a year or two with the date of the Nativity as arrived at from other calculations.

Wherever the story of the Wise Men came from it is unlikely that the writer invented it. Such legends are usually based on real events that have developed in the course of time, with gaps filled in and suitable details added. The original story of the visit to Herod's court might have come from someone who had been at the court at the time, who told it to S.Matthew himself or to whomsoever passed it on orally or wrote it down. It is enough for us that astronomy suggests that the story of such a visit from the East is entirely possible.

For the rest of the story we can only speculate, and it is here that we can see the likelihood of an Essene connexion. The similarity between the teaching of Jesus and that of the Essenes is so striking that it is not unreasonable to suppose Jesus was in some way a protégé of theirs. The Essenes were anxious to see the return to power of the house of David, to restore to the Jews an independence in their own country for which they had yearned more often than enjoyed, a real independence to replace the rule of a king of foreign family subject to the authority and support of the Roman Emperor.

From what little we know of him, Joseph could well have been an Essene craftsman – one of those living normal lives in the community but in accordance with Essene rules. He was, as far as we can tell, a man of good repute and unimpeachable lineage, being a direct descendant of the Jewish king, David. Who better than he to be the father of the future Saviour of the Jews? In the gospel story an angel spoke to Joseph in a dream – some explanation had to be given for Joseph's decision. In reality it could have been a messenger from the Essenes, clad in their regular white garb, sent to tell him what he had been selected to do. There were among the Essenes maidens, often unwanted orphans rescued by them, dedicated to the service of God, something like the Roman vestal virgins. Mary was probably one of these, a kind of nun vowed to celibacy. But the vow of celibacy was not absolute: there was a duty to ensure the survival of the Jewish people, and, in this case, of the House of David. The story as told by Matthew may hide the truth beneath a thin veneer of legend: Mary was selected to be the mother of the son that Joseph would father, and under the command of the Essene priests they were betrothed. This betrothal would, normally, have lasted three years; but whether it was by special command or by human weakness, Joseph gave Mary a child before the marriage had been finalized. He would feel some shame when Mary became pregnant, but the Essene authorities, being anxious that there should be a child, told them not to be ashamed. Joseph then completed his marriage and Jesus was thus born legitimate, the heir to the royal line of David. An alternative is also possible. Mary may have been told to accept the seed of an anonymous Essene priest, by whom she became pregnant, and Joseph was then chosen as her husband to give Jesus an official father from the house of David. When told to wed her he may not have been aware that she was already with child, and, until the matter was explained to him naturally hesitated to take Mary as his wife. The weakness of this possibility is that Jesus would not then have been a real descendant of David, the Essenes would know he wasn't, and when he reached manhood he might have discovered the truth for himself.

Matthew does not say that Joseph went to Bethlehem, "the city of David" for the birth, but only that it was there that Jesus was born to fulfil the Messianic prophecies, which Matthew continually emphasized to support the claim that Jesus was the Messiah. For the same reason the Essenes would have made sure that it was there the birth took place, whatever was the normal home of Joseph at the time.

The flight to Egypt was also very possibly Essene inspired. There was an Essene community in Alexandria, but tradition has it that it was to the village of Mataria, on the east bank of the Nile, that Joseph went. There were Jews there who tended a garden of balsam plants which Cleopatra had brought back from Jericho a little over thirty years earlier. There is a church of the Holy Family there today, and the tradition that the family did stay there is a very ancient one, which strengthens the probability that Matthew's story is based on fact. Herod died in 4BC, only a couple or so of years after the probable visit of the Wise Men. Matthew does not specify how long after that date the family returned to Palestine, but as Archelaus was still in Judea at the time it could not have been later than AD6, when he was deposed.

Matthew states that Joseph then settled in Nazareth. As already explained, Nazareth may not have existed at the time, and the assumption that it was to Nazareth that Joseph went on his return from Egypt may be due to his confusing the name of Nazareth with the prophecy that the Messiah should be called a Nazarene or Nazarite – a term denoting a holy man practising celibacy, not a man from Nazareth. If Jesus lived in Nazareth one more Messianic prophecy would have been fulfilled, so for Matthew Nazareth it had to be.

The birth story according to Luke is very different except that Luke agrees that the birth of Jesus took place in Bethlehem during the reign of Herod, confirming the location and the approximate date.

In Luke's story, also, messages were brought by "angels", but in very different circumstances. It seems that S.Luke (if it was he who wrote the story) knew the outline of what happened, and filled in the gaps as he thought appropriate. He tells how Gabriel (an "archangel" – one of the most important angels) visited Mary, a virgin engaged to Joseph, a descendant of David, and told her that through the power of God, although she was a virgin, she had been specially chosen to give birth to a son who would be called the Son of God and who would inherit the throne of David (which meant being King of the Jews).

The truth may be that the "angels" (which means "messengers") were messengers sent to Mary from the Essenes, as suggested for the story told by Matthew. If brought up by the Esssenes and dedicated to God's service, Mary would have accepted their authority, and whatever they commanded she would have considered the will of God.

It is has already been mentioned that S.Luke is said to have met Mary in her old age; if true she could have told him what happened: she could have explained that she received a message from God to be the mother of Joseph's child, and S.Luke would have pictured this as it appears in his gospel. But more probably the story was told by Mary to others, who passed it on to S.Luke, which would better explain its final divergence in detail from the now lost truth. The gospels give no description of the messengers called "angels": it is only because of their later portrayal over centuries of religious art that we tend to think of them as human-like beings with wings and haloes.

According to Luke, Mary and Joseph were already living in Nazareth when the first message came – an assumption based, no doubt, on the same misunderstanding of the term "Nazarene" as that made by Matthew. That the messenger was identified as the Archangel Gabriel was doubtless assumed because of the importance of the message.

As Luke places Joseph's home in Nazareth he has to find some way to explain why he went to Bethlehem for the birth. For this he uses the requirements of a census. But there is no record in Roman history of such a census at that time: and had there been one it is highly improbable that people would have had to register in a town some seventy-five miles away as the crow flies from where they lived because of some ancestral connexion there. There would have been Jews travelling all over Palestine if this had been necessary since the rule would apply to everyone, not just to Joseph, about whom the Romans knew nothing. It is far more probable that Joseph, wherever he lived at the time, had been told by the Essenes to make sure his son was born in Bethlehem in order to establish his claim to the position intended for him, or – and this seems equally probable – since Jesus was born in the spring (shepherds had their flocks out at night at the time) Joseph was on his way to Jerusalem for the Passover, and had reached Bethlehem when the time for the birth arrived, and when Jerusalem and nearby villages were crowded with pilgrims. In these circumstances, that "there was no room at the inn" was very probable, and Jesus may well have been born in an outhouse used for cattle or for the donkeys of wayfarers.

When Mary was delivered of her child, as a dedicated virgin used to the hymns and psalms of the Essenes, it would have been natural for her to give thanks by using one of them – one that we now call the *Magnificat* (Lk 1,46), and in later life told others that she had done so. The *Magnificat* as given by Luke is not among any of the Essene hymns that have so far come to light, but its sentiments, based on the psalms and other verses from the Old Testament, are typical of Essene hymns, and it may be one now lost, known to S.Luke, or composed by him from elements common to others. Its inclusion in the gospel strengthens the belief that Mary was, herself, an Essene dedicated to the service of God.

In Luke's story, after the birth of Jesus, there were shepherds nearby watching their sheep, whom an angel visited, telling them of the birth of the Messiah. For the Essenes who had arranged the marriage of Joseph and Mary, who had watched when it was known that she was to be a mother, and who had anxiously awaited the outcome of the birth in the hope that her child would be a boy, it appeared that what they had planned had occurred: an heir to the throne of David had been born who was destined to be the Saviour of Israel, the Messiah. A party of white-robed Essenes had visited Bethlehem and confirmed the birth, and on their way back to Jerusalem were so full of the good news that when they came across some shepherds watching their sheep they could not resist telling them the good news. The shepherds, simple men, unused to anyone passing their way by night, when they were thus greeted with such news by these enthusiastic men in white, felt that they, surely, must be angels – did not their Scriptures speak of such events having happened in the past? And now, here it was, happening to them! The truth needed but little embellishment to become the story told by Luke.

When Mary received her instruction she was also told about Elizabeth, the mother of John the Baptist. Luke does not tell us where Elizabeth lived beyond saying that it was in the hill country of Judea, which suggests that in actual fact Joseph may at that time have been living in the same area, not in Galilee.

The story of the conception of John the Baptist, a relative of Jesus, like that of Jesus, involves angelic intervention, but how much is based on fact is equally doubtful. As in the case of Jesus, S.Luke may not have invented the entire story, but may have assumed too much from what little he really knew. It would have seemed unquestionable to him, as also to those from whom he obtained his information, that if Jesus, the incarnate Son of God, was to have a forerunner, then the forerunner must have had an appropriately prestigious birth, and the story may have thus evolved through the process of filling in the gaps, an art at which the author of Luke excelled.

The main story of the Baptist, his condemnation of Herod's marital infidelity and consequent execution is supported by Josephus as well as by Luke; and there seems good evidence to believe he was a practising and even a fanatical ascetic Essene. If so, knowing that Mary's son Jesus had been prepared to inherit the throne of David, it would have been natural that he should greet Jesus as one greater than himself. Whether, had he lived, he would have become a rival rather than a follower of Jesus it is impossible to say. He certainly had a large number of followers at the time of his death, and lacked the moderation and humanity of Jesus.

Such, then, are the two accounts, each with its elements of possible, perhaps probable, truth.

After the birth of Jesus Mary's status would have remained that of a dedicated virgin. Together with Joseph, to her care were entrusted the childhood years of Jesus, he who was destined when he reached manhood, after the necessary years of training, to fulfil the mission allotted to him.

Brought up as an orthodox Jew, Jesus would have been circumcised a week after his birth, when his name would have been given. (Luke 2,21). Then, forty days after giving birth Mary had to go to the Temple for "purification" (Luke 2,22), when Jesus was "presented". According to Luke it was then that the family returned to Nazareth. Luke doubtless assumed that this is what must have happened. Having brought them to Bethlehem from Nazareth he now had to get them back again (Lk 2,39). But Luke appears to have known nothing of the Wise Men, nor of the flight to Egypt, and his apparent ignorance of these events (which in themselves seem highly probable) make it even more unlikely that he did obtain information from Mary herself. Had he done so he would have known that the real reason that Joseph went north to Galilee was not to return home, shortly after the birth of Jesus, but to avoid living under Archelaus, as Matthew tells us (Mtt 2,22). A heavenly "messenger" would have known better; some casual traveller from Palestine might not. Matthew, whose sources seem to have been better chosen than Luke's, was nearer the truth.

Archelaus was, in fact, so obnoxious that even the Romans could not stomach him and threw him out in AD6, putting his provinces under the interim control of the governor of Syria, Quirinius. It was then, about the time when it thus became safe for Jesus, as a boy of about 12, to appear in Jerusalem in public (and not at his birth), that a census (Luke 2,3) actually took place. Luke, with typical disregard for such details as dates, with only the vaguest information about this census, had snatched on it as an apparently suitable reason for bringing Joseph to Bethlehem, whereas in all probability it did not affect in any way the movements of Joseph and his family.

What Matthew does not tell us is how long the stay in Egypt lasted, but there would have been no reason to go north to Galilee after Archelaus was removed in AD6. All we are told, and this by Luke, is that at the age of twelve, that is about that year, on a visit to Jerusalem with his parents, Jesus remained behind in the Temple, where his parents eventually found him amazing the Jewish teachers there with his questions and answers. This would not be so surprising if, as is possible, Jesus had spent his early formative years under Essene instruction, acquiring wisdom and learning – wisdom and learning, incidentally, that owed much to the Essene contacts with Buddhism.

There could have been another, very practical reason, for Joesph's going to Galilee on his return from Egypt. The destruction of Sepphoris, mentioned in Chapter II) took place in AD4. Many of the inhabitants who survived may have taken refuge in what then became the new town of Nazareth, some five miles away. Joseph was a carpenter, and on returning to Palestine would have wanted work; there would have been plenty of work there, in Nazareth. This is pure supposition, but it fits known facts and the Nazareth tradition. A new town did appear during the lifetime of Jesus, a place where Joseph the Carpenter is supposed to have lived.

Once Archelaus was out of the way there was no further danger in a visit by Jesus to Jerusalem, supposing that Archelaus had known of his existence and why that existence had so alarmed his father. Thus, when Jesus was twelve years old he could safely visit Jerusalem and there be received into his own religious community in some ceremony similar to the Jewish bar-mitzvah, when a boy takes on full religious responsibility. Although the official priesthood of the Temple was provided by the Sadducees, other sects used the Temple as well, and at that time the leaders of the Essenes were in Jerusalem. Doubtless the early upbringing of Jesus had been monitored, and now that he was twelve years old it was time to ascertain how suitable he was for training for the task for which he was destined. According to Luke (Lk 2,43) he remained in the Temple when his parents started off on the way home.

The words with which, as Luke records them, Jesus rebuked his worried parents when he was found, seem to suggest that this was deliberate: "Did you not know that I must be in my Father's house?" The question may appear harsh in the brief telling of the event, but it could have been a way to remind Joseph that Jesus was intended for higher things than the usual destiny of a son to follow in his father's footsteps.

That Jesus started his mission in Galilee seems reasonably certain, but over twenty-five years were to pass between this visit to Jerusalem and the start of his public life at the age of about thirty-six or more – years about which we know nothing.

These are the hidden years, years which even S.Luke makes no attempt to fill beyond telling us that Jesus grew in body and in wisdom, gaining favour with God and man (Luke 3,52).

In the ordinary course of things Jesus, as a young child, would have been taught the Jewish Scriptures and Jewish law, and would have become acquainted with Hebrew, the language of most of the Scriptures. He would have learnt to read and write, and we are told that he was accustomed, during his mission, to read from and comment on the Scriptures to the congregation in the local synagogue. By that time he had the standing of a Rabbi (he is reported to have been so addressed on several occasions), this being, at that time, a term of respect used by students for their teachers and did not mean that Jesus was a sort of clergyman. His knowledge of the Scriptures was considerable: he often quoted from them. Although probably not learnt in the local "school", he doubtless also had at least a working knowledge of Koine, the popular form of Greek used throughout the provinces of the Roman Empire that bordered the eastern Mediterranean, and he may have used it when speaking to people who were not native Galileans, such as Roman officers and Syrians.

There would have been no danger of being recruited into the Roman army. Although it was largely recruited locally from conscripts, the Jews themselves were excused this duty as their religion, which forbade their working or carrying arms on the Sabbath, made their employment impracticable, besides which the Jews were too resentful of the Roman presence in their country to have been considered either useful or reliable.

If indeed an Essene community had entrusted Jesus to Joseph for something more than an ordinary upbringing, once his bar-mitzvah was over he would have had to undergo special training for his future role. This training would have been arranged by the Essene authorities who had planned for his future.

Again, if the Buddhist tradition is correct – and there is evidence that it is – some of those years of preparation were spent in Kashmir under Buddhist tutelage. There would have been plenty of groups of traders travelling to India and other parts of the near East with whom Jesus as a youth could have travelled in safety, until he could be handed over to his spiritual teachers. That Jesus went to India is suggested by the apocryphal Gospel of the Hebrews – the suggestion is no new idea. That he did so is also borne out by ancient Tibetan and Indian writings. The evidence for this is given in great detail by Professor Fida Hassnain in his book "A Search for the Historical Jesus". It is highly improbable that Jesus just lived quietly in Galilee for twenty-five years or so as an ordinary craftsman – a carpenter like his father – and then suddenly emerged as a fully-fledged teacher and healer. The belief that Jesus spent those years mainly in India makes sense when one compares the similarities between his teaching and that of the Essenes on one hand, and of the Buddhists on the other. The records of the Buddhists state that he not only studied among them but was also accepted by them as a teacher.

The legend that he visited Glastonbury is just a legend – but it could be based on truth like so many other legends. If Jesus went to the East with merchants he may also have joined one – tradition says Joseph of Arimathea – on a trading journey to Britain, where the Phoenicians, from the province just north of Galilee, regularly sailed to obtain tin from Cornwall. Certainly he could have returned from India with time enough to make such a journey which Professor Hassnain, supporting the theory, suggests might have been in AD25-27, when Jesus was in his early thirties, not long before his mission in Palestine began.

In his final months of training Jesus and his cousin John the Baptist may have undergone some training together, or Jesus may have been put under the Baptist's tutelage. As a dedicated ascetic and already a successful popular "man of God" it may have been the hope of John's Essene masters that such training would give Jesus the thrust to launch him into the role planned for him. John practised the Essene custom of baptism, and Jesus's mission started – was planned to start – with his being baptized by John – to present him to John's followers as The One for whom John had been preparing them.

Those who had chosen Jesus as the legitimate heir to the throne of David would have envisaged him in the role of Messiah Saviour of Israel. It would have been for this they planned his preparation, and for this the Baptist seems to have welcomed him. But things did not work out as planned. In the first place, John was executed. This might have enhanced the position of Jesus had he been like John. But he was not. He had a deeper and more realistic vision, a vision of God's plan for mankind that soared far above the ideal of worldly material conquest which dominated the thoughts of the oppressed Jewish subjects of the Roman province of Palestine. He was very far from being the leader of men as the Essenes must have visualized him. His years among the Buddhist monks of the Tibet borderland had taught him gentler ways. He did not dream of an army to overthrow the Romans; he did not wish to preach about the wickedness of kings and governors. He did not wish, after a period of retreat, to live the life of an ardent, fanatical ascetic. The kingdom of God, his kingdom, would not be like that of David his ancestor, a kingdom achieved by force of arms, by death and destruction. He saw the kingdom as the rule of God in the hearts of men, and from the moment he set forth on his own he followed the gentler path which the Essenes, perhaps unwittingly, had taught him.

As in the story of Lazarus who came forth from the tomb wrapped round in his burial shroud, Jesus stepped forth out of the bondage of Jewish thought to preach his own saving message.

Since the Essenes were by reputation peace-loving, since they did not believe in violence, it may seem improbable that they would have planned to promote someone as King of the Jews to overthrow the Romans. But there had been for a hundred years or more before the birth of Jesus, as the Dead Sea Scrolls show, a belief that in some miraculous way the Jews, as his chosen people, would be freed by the hand of God from Roman rule, and win once more an independent sovereign state under their own king. This deliverance from bondage would be not only for the two tribes of Israel that were the existing inhabitants of Palestine, but would somehow include the ten "lost" tribes – all the descendants of Israel. The achievement of this victorious work of God would be assisted by the angels under the Archangel Michael. This belief is reflected in the teaching of Jesus when he speaks of the "Kingdom of God", and it was reflected in the belief of the early church that Jesus would soon return and establish his kingdom, and all mankind would be subjected to his rule.

Unfortunately for the world he was executed before his message was properly understood, and the old Jewish eschatological ideas continued to dominate the outlook of his first followers, who formed the early Church.

If the birth of Jesus had been contrived by Essenes as suggested, the origins of both birth stories as we now have them are not too difficult to explain as legends based on fact. It is also possible, as an alternative, as already suggested, that both stories were later inventions written and added to the gospels in order to provide evidence for the belief in the divinity of Jesus which the original texts did not contain. There are words and phrases used in Matthew's birth story that are not used elsewhere, which suggest that it is by a different hand from the main body of the text. The genealogy is clearly a later addition added with the intention of showing that Jesus was descended from David, and the birth story could have been similarly added.

If this theory that the birth of Jesus was contrived by Essenes to provide the Jews with a Davidic leader, though attractive, is wrong, this does not make less likely that the visit of Jesus to India during young manhood did take place. It could have done so naturally enough. Trade routes existed; trade with both the East and the West was well established. As a young man Jesus could easily have had the opportunity to join a caravan going to India. Once there he would have met Buddhists teachers; he would not have been the first Jewish traveller to study in their monasteries. It may have been for that very reason that he made the journey, hungering after wisdom, or he may have joined a caravan simply for the experience, and discovered the wisdom of the East on arrival. It certainly seems that he independently evolved his own conception of the Kingdom of God and the role of Judaism in the wider world of which he had considerably more understanding than his stay-at-home fellow countrymen. In either case he would have returned home with another caravan of merchants, and perhaps then met and impressed Joseph of Arimathea, who was to play such an important part at the time of his crucifixion.

After his baptism by John, Jesus set out to preach the Kingdom of God as he conceived it. There was going to be no overthrow of Rome, no new independent Jewish kingdom because his kingdom was the kingdom of God, of God who was equally creator of all mankind, all mankind being his sons and daughters, regardless of race or place. It was a vision new to Jewish thought, too radical for even his closest followers to grasp; a vision which disappointed the narrow expectations of some of them. Among the followers of Jesus there were at least two who belonged to the more bellicose of the Galileans, Simon the Zealot and Judas Iscariot. Their sympathies and their hopes lay with active revolutionaries rather than with the pacific Essenes. When he saw that Jesus was willing to submit without a struggle Judas Iscariot tried to force his Master to take a more adversarial stand. But Jesus held to his vision, the fruit of years of study and of ascetic living and meditation. When, at the end of his mission, he was presented to the Romans as one who claimed to be King of the Jews, one who would overthrow the ruling power, the accusation was all too clearly a travesty of the truth. It is not surprising that even Pilate, a man of most unpleasant reputation, could find no cause to condemn him, but did so only as a matter of political expediency.

The Jesus that emerges from the gospel accounts of his final mission, his trial and execution, is that of an accomplished teacher, a man of prayer and learning, a man of deep human understanding, a man of peace, a devout servant of God – but indubitably a man like other men, a man of his own time, of his own race, but not the Messiah and King the Essenes had hoped for. Although Jesus would not restore to the Jews the kingdom of David his vision went beyond the confines of their own small corner of the earth, beyond the brief period of their own lifetime, beyond the narrow bounds of the Hebrew race – one whose vision surpassed all such narrow bounds, one whose "kingdom of God" was to be for all men and for all time. His vision has become so much a part of western culture, of civilization as we know it, that it is difficult to appreciate how far in advance it was of the ideals and aspirations of the Jews in particular, and mankind in general, two thousand years ago.

Judas Iscariot's effort to force the hand of Jesus ended in disaster. Jesus was arrested and Iscariot himself committed suicide in despair. The followers of Jesus deserted him, and all seemed lost when

Jesus was condemned to die by crucifixion. But he had friends who were determined to save him, friends who, perhaps, had known him longer than his recently acquired disciples, friends who knew his true worth, and who better understood what he stood for. Their names are known to us. They were Joseph of Arimathea and Nicodemus, Pharisees and merchants of repute.

CHAPTER VII
CRUCIFIXION – RESURRECTION OR RESUSCITATION?

The central doctrine of orthodox Christianity is not the manner of his birth but the belief that Jesus died by being crucified, and that on the third day after his death "rose again from the dead". Unlike the birth stories, all four gospels give a detailed account of the crucifixion and the "death" of Jesus, and though they vary in detail they agree on this essential fact. All four gospels follow their account of his death with a somewhat confused and different account of his resurrection and subsequent appearances. The account given by Matthew is very brief; there are alternative endings for Mark, one of which is even shorter.

S.Paul, in his first epistle to the Corinthians, declared that without the resurrection faith in salvation through the death of Jesus was in vain. The resurrection forms a key element in his teaching (1 Cor, 15,17): it was the conquest of death by Jesus that was the guarantee of future bliss in the life to come for all who believed.

But did it really happen? Did Jesus really "rise from the dead"?

There is a considerable amount of misconception about the meaning of the word "resurrection", often confused with "resuscitation". "Resuscitation" means bringing back to conscious life someone who is unconscious or apparently dead as the result of some respiratory or cardiac failure, as, for example, when someone has been nearly drowned, or after a heart attack, or as the result of electrocution. The "kiss of life", heart massage, and electric shock treatment are the best known and possibly most frequently used methods of achieving resuscitation. There is nothing miraculous or abnormal about the results of such treatment. A person who has been resuscitated has been brought back from the brink of death, but has not actually crossed the final, normally un-recrossable, line that separates life from death: but in individual cases exactly where the frontier lies is not always clear.

"Resurrection" does not mean restoring to conscious life someone apparently dead, someone who may have been incorrectly diagnosed as dead. It means restoring to life someone who has completely severed all links with the living world – as dead as a lifeless corpse can be. The resurrection of Jesus, in orthodox theology, is the forerunner of the resurrection on the Last Day of every human person who by then will have died, restored to life in the same bodies as they had in their natural lifetime, but a body without its imperfections. The wicked as well as the good will rise, but sin will make the bodies of the wicked hideous and repulsive. Thus the doctrine of the resurrection does not refer to the mere survival of the soul in a spiritual non corporeal state, which is probably what most people consider to be what happens if there is life after death.

The "resurrection" of Jesus in its correct theological sense means that he retained a living body, the same body as he had before he died, but while it was materially the same body it underwent a miraculous change so that it no longer had the normal weaknesses and limitations of a human body; it was without its former natural material limitations.

For resurrection to take place, death must first occur. The fact of actual death is a prerequisite for a true resurrection.

The arguments in support of the belief that Jesus did actually die on the cross are not without weight, but they leave unanswered a number of questions which cannot be avoided, and which can only be answered satisfactorily by accepting the alternative theory: that Jesus did not die on the cross, but recovered from the ordeal.

On careful examination it will be found that the theory that Jesus did not die on the cross, but was taken down alive and subsequently recovered, is supported even by much of the evidence offered by the gospels themselves. The theory is no new one: it dates back to the beginning of Christianity, and was part of the belief of early "heretical" Christian sects – an old tradition that continued to be held for many centuries and was adopted by the Koran, the holy book of Islam, in the early seventh century. According to the gospels – and all four agree on all the main points – Jesus was executed by crucifixion. That a crucifixion did take place seems incontrovertible. Even those who deny the resurrection do not usually dispute the fact, though one explanation was that someone else was substituted for Jesus, and one scholar has recently postulated that he was, in fact, stoned to death (J. Enoch Powell, *The Evolution of the Gospel*). Brief references to Jesus in the writings of contemporary non-Christian Roman historians mention the crucifixion. Crucifixion was very frequently used at that time by the Romans when executing people of the many subject races in the Roman Empire, but it was not used for those who were classed as "Roman citizens" – a status granted to many who were not by birth Romans, including S.Paul. As far as Jesus was concerned, he was in the eyes of the Romans a revolutionary-minded agitator, just another of those troublesome Galileans. At least, that is how the Jews who accused him presented him to the Roman authorities, knowing that was the best way to get rid of him, and that crucifixion would be his inevitable fate. It must be made clear here that it was Jews who accused Jesus with the object of getting rid of him; but it was not "the Jews" as a people. Jesus was himself a Jew; his followers were Jews and so were his enemies – he lived among Jews, so it was natural enough that in the world in which he lived it would be mainly Jews who were both his friends and his foes. His Jewish enemies were those who feared for their own position, the ruling Sadducees, who wanted his death because they saw in the success of Jesus a threat to their position as the controllers of the Temple, a position recognized by the Roman authorities and which they jealously guarded. When, during the Middle Ages, Jews were condemned as a race guilty of the death of Jesus it was overlooked that Christianity as a religion is Jewish in its origins; two thirds of the Christian Bible are shared with and inherited from the Jews; its central doctrine of monotheism is of Jewish origin; much of its forms of worship are Jewish – the psalms, for instance; and all its earliest followers and propagators were Jews. The "ten commandments" which in England frequently appear on screens in parish churches and which at one time children learnt by heart were the commandments given by Moses to the Jews. The shameful treatment of Jews in the Middle Ages was, sadly, as unchristian as it was unjust.

Because, under Roman rule, the Jews themselves were not entitled to carry out crucifixions, to make sure Jesus would be executed they had to persuade the Romans it was in their interests to get rid of him. The Sadducees might have tried to have him stoned to death, but even for this the acquiescence of the Romans would probably have been necessary; and they were probably alarmed by the great number of Jesus's Galilean followers who had, a few days previously, flocked triumphantly into Jerusalem to celebrate the Passover there. Successfully to stone him to death would require the general support of the crowds: and they had not yet discovered how fickle the crowds supporting Jesus would prove to be. They knew that there were close friends of Jesus among the Galileans; and they could not be sure what attitude the many other pilgrims in the city who knew nothing of Jesus might adopt towards him. It was thus far from certain whether a decision to stone Jesus to death would have been successful. Crucifixion was safer, and would put responsibility for the death, and the burden of any unpopularity, on the shoulders of the occupying power.

Crucifixion involved being nailed through the wrists to a wooden beam placed on the ground: this beam was then fixed to a post to which the feet were then nailed, after which the whole structure in the shape of a giant "T" was raised to an upright position and planted in a hole already prepared in the ground. If the body were left to hang from the wrists death occurred quickly from suffocation and heart failure; but the Romans intended the death to be slow and painful. To ensure that the torment lasted longer than a few hours a sort of seat, the *sedile*, in the form of a block of wood, was sometimes attached to the upright. On this the victim could rest, taking the weight off his wrists. An alternative, with the same intention, was a support under the feet, to which they were nailed. This, the *suppedaneum*, enabled the victim to raise himself on his straightened legs to relieve the weight on his wrists. At first sight these supports may seem like efforts to make crucifixion less painful. It is human nature to try to avoid death and pain, and victims could not resist the momentary relief which the *sedile* or the *suppedaneum* offered. The unhappy and intended result was, however, the prolongation of the torture; and where they were in use death usually did not occur until after several days of agony. In the case of Jesus, and of the two thieves crucified with him, it is clear that the *suppedaneum* was used, because the soldiers had to break the legs of the two thieves to make it impossible for them to stand, thus hastening their death – breaking their legs would have been pointless if the *sedile* had been in use. This apparent act of mercy was, on this occasion, performed not to shorten their suffering but because the execution took place on the Friday which was the eve of the feast of the Passover Sabbath, and the Jewish authorities did not want the bodies to remain on the crosses throughout the festival holy day, which started at sundown. It was fortunate for Jesus that the crucifixion took place on that particular day: normally the victims would have been left to die slowly over the course of two or three days; as it was the circumstances made it necessary for the whole procedure to be limited to about five hours. Had the Romans had any real reason for the execution of Jesus, had they regarded him as a danger to the Empire and to their control of Palestine, they might have been less ready to acquiesce in the wishes of the Jewish priests. But as far as they were concerned he was less of a danger than the two petty thieves they were executing with him, and so were quite prepared to do what the priests requested. There were too many people, full of religious fervour, crowded into Jerusalem to risk upsetting their tiresome religious sensitivities.

The Last Supper which Jesus shared with his disciples, and which is celebrated in the majority of Christian churches as the Mass, Eucharist or Holy Communion, was not the normal Passover meal, which would have taken place on the Friday when the Pascal lamb was eaten. The crucifixion took place on the Friday – of that there can be no question. Moreover, as far as can be known from the description given in the gospels, no lamb was eaten, the meal consisting of bread. That was to be expected if Jesus and his companions followed the Essene custom, which was to have bread at their "Passover". Moreover, the Essenes kept the festival on the Wednesday, using a different calendar. Although the traditional day for the Last Supper is Thursday, if it took place on Wednesday there would have been more time for all the events to happen which took place between that evening and the morning of the crucifixion.

We know, if the testimony of all four gospels is to be relied upon, that after the Last Supper there was at least one night when Peter denied knowing Jesus (John, 18,22 – the synoptics also tell this story), and the following morning Jesus was mocked by the guards, appeared before the Sanhedrin (the chief priests and elders). Caiphas, the chief priest, also spent some time examining witnesses. Jesus was then taken to Pilate. As Jesus was a Galilean, Pilate sent him to Herod Antipas, ethnarch of Galilee who happened to be in Jerusalem; who questioned him with interest, but when Jesus refused to speak or work a miracle he was again mocked and sent back to Pilate (Luke, 22, 66ff) where after further interrogation he was flogged and the crown of thorns (actually a sort of cap) was placed mockingly on his head. The crowd was asked if Jesus should be the prisoner chosen to be released in accordance with a Passover custom, but the crowd shouted for Barabbas (convicted of murder and riot). Jesus was then handed over to the soldiers to be taken out of the city.

All this must have taken a long time; it could not have happened in one morning, almost certainly not in one day. It is probable that the Supper was, therefore, on the Wednesday and these events took place on the Thursday and Friday morning.

Mark says that Jesus was nailed to the cross at the "third hour" (nine o'clock in the morning: Mk 15, 25) but this is certainly inaccurate. The synoptics agree that there was darkness over the land from noon to three o'clock (sixth to ninth hours), and that seems to be the approximate time they intended to indicate that Jesus was on the cross before he lost consciousness, and was thought to be dead.

The gospels give somewhat differing accounts of what else happened. Matthew contains a highly imaginative description of an earthquake and graves opening and people rising from the dead and going into Jerusalem, which, had it happened, would hardly have escaped the notice of more serious historians, and would have left some archaeological evidence as well. Matthew's account seems, at least in part. to be another case of adapting the facts to fit the words of the Hebrew Scriptures, in this case Psalm 18, 4-7: "The sorrows of death compassed me ... in my distress I called upon the Lord ... then the earth shook and trembled". The centurion and his soldiers are said to have witnessed everything that happened; but some of these events took place "after Jesus had risen" (Mtt 27,53) – thus the soldiers could not have witnessed them at the moment of Jesus's death. Mark gives a less dramatic account, describing how the veil in the Temple was torn in two at the moment of Jesus's death, as does Luke. John does not mention any of these dramatic phenomena, but gives a much more detailed account of the scene at the foot of the cross (John, 19,16ff) which reads as if it were based on first-hand memories. With the exception of S.John and the faithful women (John 19,25) none of the other disciples of Jesus are reported as having been close at hand during the crucifixion of their Master. They may have gathered, anxiously, safely out of the way, as suggested by Luke's vague statement that "all who had known him, including the women who had followed him from Galilee, stood at a distance." (Luke 23,49). This strengthens the theory that the gospel attributed to S.John intended to correct the somewhat imaginary accounts of the other gospels, already circulating when John was written. Some slight later editing of the text of John doubtless took place; the references to prophecies could have been added as explanatory "foot-notes". When comparing all their accounts of what happened when Jesus is supposed to have died, John's account is credible – that of Matthew is not.

If Jesus was not actually raised on the cross until towards 1 o'clock he had been on it less than three hours by the "ninth hour" (three o'clock) when it was thought he died. This would have been too short a time for death to have taken place, but the drink given him on a sponge may have been a narcotic to help him lose consciousness, which made it appear that he had died. He would then not have been able to support himself on his legs, and if he was to be rescued it was necessary to remove him as soon as possible. It must have been no more than an hour or so later that the legs of the two other victims were broken to hasten their death, so that the bodies could be removed well before sundown at 6 o'clock, when the Sabbath began.

The soldiers did not break Jesus's legs. The reason given by John (19,33) was that they found him already dead. The simple statement of the gospels that Jesus died has been accepted without question by orthodox Christian teaching; it is, however, improbable that a man as fit as Jesus would, in fact, have died so soon while the two thieves crucified with him remained alive for yet some time – until their death had to be hastened by the breaking of their legs. It could be argued that once Jesus lost consciousness he hung from his wrists as if his legs had been broken. There is, however, a difference: if he was under the effect of a drug this would have had a calming effect on his heart, and he would not have needed to breathe so deeply, reducing the danger of heart-failure or strangulation. Whether or not this is the explanation, there is evidence to show that Jesus was not dead. This evidence is simple enough: the account as given by John goes on to say that "one of the soldiers pricked Jesus's side with a spear". The Greek verb used for "pricked" is *nusso*, which means to touch lightly with a sharp point, to prick or nudge in an exploratory manner. The usual translation in English texts is "pierced": and the "Good News" version uses "plunged" – an example of how easily a bad translation may mislead. The verb *nusso* is not used elsewhere, and must have been deliberately chosen: it was not intended to describe a "death stroke" but a probe to see if Jesus was still alive. Three verses later a quotation from the Scriptures is given in which the verb is *ekkenteo*, which can mean "stab": "They shall look upon him whom they have pierced" (Zechariah 12,10). It is probable that this and other quotations given here are "footnotes", added to the original text, otherwise the original author would surely have chosen the same verb as his quotation had he wished to link the one with the other.

Following the "pricking" "immediately water and blood came out". Jesus would not have bled from the wound had he been dead. His blood must have still been circulating. If it is true that S.John was present and was the source of this information (as the text itself claims), the emphasis laid upon this phenomenon suggests that it was a fact of some significance – although its full significance seems to have escaped him. John says that both "blood and water" came from the wound – the "water" could have been the fluid that would have collected in the peritoneal cavity (so some opinions state). The liturgical practice at the celebration of the Last Supper of mixing the communion wine with water recalls this. The use of the word "immediately" implies that "blood gushed forth freely", not as a weak momentary ooze that might have appeared after death. It seems likely that the centurion in command would have known that bleeding meant life was not extinct, and his apparent acquiescence with the request by Joseph of Arimathea and Nicodemus – the two powerful (possibly Essene-friendly) friends of Jesus – to allow them to remove the body while still alive, can only be explained by his shutting his eyes to the facts. It may be he was bribed; it is preferable to believe, as some early traditions have it, that he admired Jesus, and that he ordered both the administration of the narcotic and the "pricking" at their request to make sure that Jesus was, in fact, not dead. The ordinary soldiers present must have been aware of the truth unless they were very inexperienced; but they would have obeyed whatever orders they were given without demur, possibly in return for a timely "consideration". Whether they were Roman soldiers or Syrian conscripts they would have had no personal interest in the affair.

This was not the only recorded occasion of a crucified victim surviving crucifixion, nor of the surrendering of a still living body on request. The historian Josephus cites the case of three victims taken down alive on request. Only one of them, however, survived the medical attention they received. The medical attention that Joseph could provide for Jesus was doubtless superior.

That the followers of Jesus – the few disciples present, the devoted women with them, and those who later were to meet the "risen" Jesus – all believed he had actually died and was "resurrected" cannot be doubted. What, however, is most certainly doubtful is whether they, whose medical knowledge was limited, could distinguish between the recovery of a person in a coma, but assumed dead, and virtual "resurrection" – the recovery of life – of someone who had actually died. There may have existed in their minds no clear distinction between a return from the brink of death and a return from having crossed that brink. The women who, on the Sunday morning, went to the tomb to anoint the body clearly expected to find him dead. It is well to note here that the traditional "three days" that Jesus is said to have lain in the tomb was in fact no more than thirty-six hours, from about sundown (6 p.m.) on Friday to sunrise on Sunday (6 a.m). It may have been less. The "third day" is only justified because parts of three different days are involved, and scarcely even that, since the Jewish day began at sundown. But the prophecies taken to refer to this spoke of three days, and three days it had to be.

The theory that Jesus's removal from the cross, and later from the tomb, was part of an Essene conspiracy can be no more than reasoned supposition. But from what we are told it seems very possible that such a conspiracy existed, and was successfully accomplished. If it is true that Jesus was looked upon by the Essenes as the representative of the house of David and the rightful leader of Jewish resistance to Roman domination, every effort to ensure his rescue and recovery would have seemed worth while, with the hope that, if he survived, the time would come when he might yet head the looked-for victory. And if rescued, then a promise that he would return to fulfil his destiny was not a hollow promise made without a reasonable expectation that it would be fulfilled within his remaining lifetime – a promise, when everyone not in the know thought he had died, which easily became transformed into the promise of the Second Coming, so eagerly and so vainly awaited by the early Christians, and still looked for in orthodox Christianity today. It is not, therefore, unreasonable to suppose that Joseph of Arimathea planned to save Jesus, using medical skills he had learned from the Essenes, whose secret disciple he could have been. That he remained nominally a Pharisee might have been of necessity. He was a merchant and a wealthy one: the Essene rules did not approve of his way of earning a living.

Under normal circumstances it would not have been Joseph of Arimathea but Jesus's mother or some near relative who would have made the arrangements for the burial, and we are told that both his mother and Mary Magdalene, a constant companion, were there at the time. That Joseph should have asked for the body indicates that he had some special plan, and the approval of the family to carry it out. That the two Marys agreed could not have been because they knew what the plan was – what happened later, on the Sunday morning, makes that much clear; but, aware that Jesus was a protégé of the Essenes and that Joseph was acting on their behalf, the women would have accepted Joseph as their nominee and left it to him to take charge, grateful, no doubt, that he was able to provide a suitable tomb. They were far from home and had to rely on someone local. Besides needing the goodwill of the centurion in charge, permission to bury the body had to be obtained from Pilate. Fortunately he seemed only too ready to appease the troublesome demands of the Jews provided he had no further trouble. The whole affair, in his eyes, was no more than a domestic quarrel among underlings. The Jews had wanted him crucified; and if they now wanted the body, what did it matter? He had quite enough on his hands with the place full of gangs of these wretched tiresome Jews streaming in for their ridiculous festival.

When Joseph took charge of his body Jesus was in a coma, and to any onlookers would have appeared dead; and it was necessary for the success of Joseph's plan that no one but his assistants should know the truth. With Nicodemus, also, we suppose, a secret Essene of some kind, and with help from two or three others, Jesus was laid in the tomb which Joseph had prepared for him. It was customary when such tombs were used for a body to remain until only the bones were left; these would then be put into a casket after which the final laying to rest would take place.

The fact that this near-by tomb was so conveniently available adds valuable evidence. Joseph did not live in Jerusalem. The whereabouts of Arimathea is uncertain, but it is thought to have been either the same as Ramah, a place five miles north of Jerusalem, or Ramathan, twenty miles to the north. In either case, Joseph would not have had his family tomb so far from home. Moreover, being a man of substance, he or his forebears would have already had a tomb in use for members of his family somewhere near his home – it would be too much of a coincidence if, by pure chance, he just happened to have recently had a new one dug for his own future use – and why so far away from his home? It is obvious that the tomb was part of the arrangements he made, and that it was intended for the one purpose for which it was used. Most likely it was not purposely dug – there would have been no time for that: but it happened to be there, as yet unused, and Joseph hired it or bought it. He may have disguised his real purpose by pretending it was for himself.

A hundred pounds of myrrh and aloes – a very large amount – had been purchased to dress the body, and must have been bought in advance, to be ready for immediate use when needed. These were not the spices usually used by the Jews to anoint a body; they were medicaments used to cure wounds. Because of the Sabbath the anointing arranged for by the women who had been at the crucifixion, and who believed Jesus to be dead, had to be delayed until early on the morning of the first day of the next week. The Sabbath ended at dusk on the Saturday, so they had to wait for daylight on the "third" day. Joseph had made sure there was a large round mill-wheel-shaped stone across the entrance, and this made the tomb secure from prying eyes, so no one would know how, and by whom, Jesus was being cared for inside. Jesus could not have been removed before early on the Sunday morning. He would need time to recover from his coma and for his wounds to be treated, and to regain enough strength to be led away. He would have to walk away, disguised – to attempt to carry him would have been too dangerous: it might look like body-snatching, and on the Sabbath would have aroused attention.

Once safely in the tomb, the comatose Jesus was laid on one end of the long linen shroud that Joseph had purchased. The wounded and scarred body was smeared with healing aloes and soothing myrrh. The end of the long shroud was drawn over his head to cover the body. Possibly the aloes had been rubbed into the cloth as well as on the body, making it a kind of giant medicinal plaster. Throughout the night and the following Saturday whoever was with Jesus watched him, and saw him recover. Just before dawn on the Sunday morning those who had tended Jesus signalled to their own guards who watched outside (Matthew, 27,65); these rolled back the stone and, still under cover of darkness, most of them quietly hurried away. Jesus, recovered but still weak, clad in garments brought for him, garments that would conceal who he was, awaited the dawn, a couple of young Essenes, wearing their typical white robes, remaining with him. Very early, before anyone else, Mary Magdalene came to the tomb with the other women, Mary the mother of James, and Salome, to anoint the body – the Jewish custom being to dress the body with oil – there was no embalming to preserve to corpse practised by the Jews. The tomb was open, the stone rolled aside, and looking in they found it empty except for the linen shroud which lay there still. A young Essene had remained with Jesus, and in Matthew (28,5) he becomes an "angel"; but Mark (16,5) says he was a young man dressed in white (Mark himself, possibly). He spoke to the women and told them Jesus was not there. That Jesus was, in fact, still there he would not want anyone to know, for safety's sake: but Jesus spoke to Mary Magdalene – she of all people had the right to know he was still alive – though until he uncovered his face she assumed he was the gardener (John 20,15).

The shroud itself was later collected and preserved, and found to have on it a negative imprint of the body of Jesus, the full value of which was only revealed when it was first photographed and the negative showed the now well-known positive image. There was nothing unusual in taking the shroud. It was a valuable strip of expensive linen. After its removal, perhaps when prepared for washing, it was discovered that there was some sort of image on it, and its value as a souvenir became apparent. People will spend hundreds and thousands of pounds for some such souvenirs – a garment, a cigar box, a chair, once owned or used by a famous person. This was the only relic of Jesus available – the Roman soldiers had already taken everything he wore (John 19,22).

It may seem strange that the Catholic Church should be anxious to disprove the authenticity of this important relic now known as the Shroud of Turin. But if the shroud is genuine it proves conclusively that Jesus was not dead as he lay on it in the tomb. The stains made by blood show that he bled from several wounds, notably from the wound in his side: that could not have happened had the body been dead. Moreover, due to the effect of *rigor mortis* a corpse could not have been in the relaxed attitude indicated by the image. The recent, modern and exhaustive scientific and medical evidence for this is overwhelming, as, indeed, is the scientific and historical evidence for the genuineness of the shroud itself. The facts are fully and lucidly explained and illustrated in *The Jesus Conspiracy* by Holger Kersten and Elmar. R Gruber and in Jesus Lived in India by Holger Kertsen (details of both are given in the Bibliography), books which are easily obtainable, and available for consultation by those who question the conclusion that it was not a "resurrection" but a "resuscitation" that accounted for the empty tomb and for Jesus's subsequent appearances.

The whole of traditional Christian theology, the very basis of the authority of the Church, depends upon the resurrection. Since the shroud, if genuine, supports resuscitation as opposed to resurrection it was necessary, in the eyes of the Church, that it be discounted – a decision it seems, arising from the same unwillingness to face truth that inspired the attack on Galileo and which gave rise to the institution of the Holy Index, which (until wisely abolished in 1966) made it a sin to read "heretical" books – that is, books that cast doubt on Catholic dogmas.

The remarkable story of the shroud – of its history, of the exhaustive modern scientific and medical evidence for its authenticity, of how the image was formed, of the flawed carbon-dating that pronounced it, unjustly and improbably, as a "fake" – is told in the two books mentioned above. Even if the carbon dating was not subjected to the manipulation they describe, the University of Texas has, more recently, stated that dust on the sample would have caused an incorrect "reading" of a genuine sample. There was also a very significant passage in *The Crucifixion by an Eye-witness* (published in Chicago in 1907, but what it said we must take on trust since most copies were destroyed). It is, fortunately, quoted at length by Professor Hassnain in his *A Search for the Historical Jesus*. The book was a translation of a Latin text of unknown authority, and purported to be an account of the crucifixion written by an Essene eye-witness seven years after the event. The passage quoted says that not only were the healing salves spread on the body and the cloth but that the aloes were used to "smoke" the tomb: this process might well have assisted in producing the image that was later found on the shroud. From evidence that the shroud itself provides, this statement appears to fit the fact of the existence of the image. Most recently, two scientists of Turin University claim to have found on the shroud, above the left eye, the faint impression of a Roman coin whose date corresponds to our AD29 – a coin placed there in accordance with Jewish custom, probably by one of the women who did not know that Jesus was still alive (reported in *The Times* of 8 June 1996).

Even without the evidence of the shroud the fact that Jesus survived the crucifixion is the only reasonable conclusion that can be drawn from consideration of such other evidence as we have. The truth of this theory of "resuscitation" does not depend on the authenticity of the shroud: but if the shroud is as genuine as the latest research shows it to be, it adds impressive supporting evidence not only for Jesus having survived the crucifixion but also for the accuracy of the descriptions given in the gospels of the treatment he suffered immediately prior to the crucifixion.

The orthodox explanation for the disappearance of Jesus's body from the tomb is that the body of the "risen" Jesus was "glorified" – that after the resurrection it was no longer subject to the laws that govern a normal physical body; and to support this is the story of how he appeared suddenly in a locked room in which the disciples were gathered (John, 20,19). But the body that Jesus had was certainly a normally physical one – he made a point of presenting it at as such: "See my hands and feet; ... feel and see: a ghost does not have flesh and bones as you see I have" (Luke, 23,30). Because the door of the room was kept locked does not mean that Jesus must have passed through the wall, as a ghost might do: a room may be kept locked to keep out unwanted strangers, but for those who are welcome the door can be opened and closed again – and if the door was opened to a knock as Jesus stood outside he would have been welcomed in with as much surprise as if he had suddenly appeared from nowhere in the middle of the room.

Jesus had been in a tomb with a heavy round stone covering the entrance. When the tomb was found empty the stone had been rolled aside – a task that had almost certainly required more than one person on the outside – the women going to the tomb were worried that they might not be able to move it; had the body of Jesus been "glorified" he could have gone out unrestricted, and the stone would have remained unmoved. In telling us that the women were worried about the stone the gospel clearly wishes to prepare us for the statement that the stone was found moved from the entrance; and this statement is likely to be correct because the disappearance of Jesus from a still closed tomb would have been in keeping with a "glorified", resurrected body; the removal of the stone is in keeping with – indeed, essential for – the disappearance of a resuscitated one.

The gospels are vague and contradictory about the appearances of Jesus after the crucifixion: but they agree that he was "real". The truth must be that he had to move about secretly, so that he would not be recognized – something that would not be difficult as he doubtless wore the usual head-scarf common in Palestine at the time and which would hide his face easily without its appearing to be done on purpose. No doubt when he joined the two disciples on the road to Emmaus (a village, it is thought, about four miles from Jerusalem) he was going, perhaps, to the safety of his friends in Bethany, keeping his head well covered, and he only revealed himself when he was sure that his two companions had been among his followers and would not betray him. Although Luke gives the impression this took place immediately after the "resurrection", Jesus may have been in hiding locally for some weeks before he ventured to make the journey. Well disguised, and sufficiently recovered from his ordeal, it would be safer in a place like Bethany than hidden in Jerusalem where he might so easily have been betrayed.

It was, of course, impossible for Jesus to continue his preaching. If it were known that he was still alive not only would he again be arrested but those who had helped him would also have been in peril. But to those he trusted he could reveal himself for brief spells, giving them directions for carrying on his mission, for it was his teaching that he wanted to promote, not himself.

It was essential for his own safety and that of Joseph, of Nicodemus and of others who had helped to rescue Jesus, to keep quiet about what had been done and where Jesus was being kept in hiding. When he did appear in public it was only to those he could trust, briefly and secretly. S.Paul, in his first letter to the Corinthians, says that Jesus appeared at one time to a group of five hundred of his followers (1 Cor 15,6). The number had doubtless been repeatedly exaggerated in re-telling by the time S.Paul heard of it, for such a gathering would have been risky to organize without the intrusion of a few informers. Had Jesus appeared before large crowds, as he had done before his arrest, he would have spoken to them, and something of what he said on such a memorable occasion would have survived, whereas more intimate meetings would have retained their privacy.

To where Jesus disappeared thereafter is not recorded. The stories of the ascension were doubtless supplied to fill the gap. That he had appeared and was known to have appeared would have alarmed those who protected him, and the decision must have been made to evacuate him beyond the reach of the Palestinian authorities. Allowed to see his followers and pass on to them his final instructions he then left them; perhaps he appeared when mists made it impossible to see where he went. He was, in any case "swallowed up" into the unknown, and as far as those in Palestine were concerned he was never seen again except, briefly, by S.Paul on his way to Damascus. Syria was outside the control of the Palestinian authorities, and there was in Damascus an Essene settlement. But even there Jesus was not safe, and he left to return to Kashmir, where he had lived and studied in the past, and where he knew he had friends. Thomas, the disciple who doubted that Jesus could have survived, was sent on in advance, and Jesus took with him his Mother, who died as they reached the border of Kashmir, and was buried at Muree. Jesus went on to the peace of Srinagar. That, at least, is what happened according to Professor Hassnain (*A Search for the Historical Jesus*), and although there are other theories this is supported by an ancient tradition, by early written evidence and by the names of places and surviving monuments, which are described by Holger Kersten and illustrated in his *Jesus Lived in India*.

The tradition that Jesus did go to India and died there is a very old one, but it has been kept away from Christians since if true it disturbs the very foundations of orthodox Christian theology. The traditional belief in both Resurrection and Ascension have been maintained although this has required glossing over when explaining in a far from satisfactory manner the inconsistencies and contradictions of the gospel stories. Suffice it to say that in the light of reason and our understanding of what a human body is, with a better understanding of what Jesus in particular actually suffered and could have lived through, the most reasonable and acceptable explanation for reports of his being seen alive after his crucifixion was that he survived the ordeal – and, if he did so, much that was not clear can be explained, the mystery of the Shroud of Turin can be unravelled, and Jesus himself can take his proper place among the great religious teachers of mankind.

On first consideration it could appear that Jesus showed a lack of courage and belief in his own teaching by disappearing. He may, indeed, have wished to remain and take up again the work he had begun, and been advised against it. Certain it is that to have remained either in Jerusalem or anywhere in Palestine would have been folly. Had he stayed openly he would have had one certain end to look forward to – a second crucifixion – and what would have been the point of undergoing the same ordeal again, for nothing – and this time with death assured? No normal human would want to go again through so traumatic an experience – one that had already all but cost him his life.

It is to be hoped that some further evidence will be found to dispel all doubt. Methods of dating bones and ancient artefacts improve with time. Recently it has been shown that the shape of the bones of a human foot can help identify the group to which its owner once belonged, and it may in time be found that Jewish bones in Muree and Srinagar confirm traditions.

Gradually, after Jesus had disappeared from Palestine and contact with him was lost, the belief that he reigned in Heaven was found a satisfactory way to explain how it was that he appeared to have no burial place. Because his eventual death, when it occurred, took place so far away to have been unknown to the nascent Church, there evolved a belief that Jesus lived – and if he lived, where but in Heaven? – and that in due course he would return in triumph to claim his kingdom, a belief that seemed reasonable enough at the time and one that has survived among many Christians to the present day.

According to S.Paul the "resurrection" of Jesus, the restoration of his life in the body after actual death, was evidence that Jesus was the incarnate Son of God. Had this been true, Jesus would have known that he would "rise again", and the gospels, under the influence of S.Paul's teaching, tried to make out that Jesus did foretell that this would happen. But Jesus did not know. If he had known or believed that he would rise again from death he would have had no reason to pray that he might be spared: he would hardly have prayed "My Father, if this be possible, take this cup away from me!" – willing though he was to obey (Mtt, 26,39; Mk, 14,36). The words of his promise to the "good thief" on the cross next to him were hardly the words of one expecting resurrection: "Today you will be in Paradise with me" (Luke, 23,43). There would have been no reason for him to commit his Mother to the care of his "beloved disciple" S.John if he knew that he would in three days be himself able to care for her (John, 19,26). Everything he is reported to have uttered when on the cross suggest that he believed he was about to die – his despairing cry "My God, my God, why have you abandoned me?" (Matt 27,46; Mk 15,34), his resigned "Father, into your hands I commend my soul" (Lk 23,46) and finally "It is finished": (John 19,30).

Whatever plans there were to save him must have been kept from him. Joseph of Arimathea was not one of his close companions, and may have had no opportunity to speak to Jesus after his arrest. The plan was a dangerous and doubtful one: its success demanded the acquiescence of the centurion in charge of the execution, if not his active connivance, and that could not be guaranteed. To Jesus himself to find he was still alive must have appeared like a miracle, just at it did to his distraught disciples when he appeared to them a few days later. As far as they were concerned, Jesus had indeed defeated death, proof that God was with him. Now it was for those whom he had prepared for the task to carry on his work. Because the difference between resurrection and resuscitation was not understood there was no fraud in their preaching the "resurrection" as they understood it.

The martyrdom of Jesus lay in the reality of the crucifixion and his all too human fear of death. He showed all the weaknesses of a very human person faced with a fearful prospect; and he showed, in spite of his fear, the dignity and submission of a man of God, and, in his last moments of agony, his consideration for his Mother and for the thief hanging on the cross at his side, were consistent with the practices and teaching of his ministry and his message for mankind.

Where Jesus finally took his leave is not clear. He must have said good-bye to different groups of followers as he moved farther from Jerusalem. S.Luke, if indeed he is responsible for both the gospel bearing his name and The Acts, locates the final appearance in two different places, the first near Bethany (Luke, 24,50), the second just outside Jerusalem, on the Mount of Olives (Acts, 1,12). Matthew (23,16) speaks of a hill in Galilee. The other gospels give no information on this point. If Jesus was being protected by his Essene friends he may have been allowed to speak to these different groups in different places, after which he was discreetly taken back into hiding. For each group he visited, the last time he was seen by them would have been for them his final appearance, and, because no one knew where he had gone his "ascension into heaven" became the accepted answer.

Can it be that the truth – that Jesus was alive but had gone to preach in the East – was known but deliberately ignored by some of the founders of the Church? Apocryphal texts, such as the Gospel of Philip and the Acts and Gospel of Thomas reveal that much was circulating among early Christians about what happened to Jesus after the "resurrection" that the gospels do not mention at all. The

Acts of Thomas speak of Jesus in the north of India, in what is now Pakistan. But if Jesus was alive the teaching of S.Paul was false, and it was the teaching of S.Paul that the early Church had adopted and wished to believe in. Can it be that there were hidden motives that made the truth unwelcome? – can it be that the brief and unsatisfactory endings of the gospels were the result of the suppression of, perhaps, politically unwise or philosophically unpalatable ideas? It would not be the only time that the Church was to be guilty of suppressing evidence that could endanger its official doctrine. Was it considered at such times better to control the minds of men with falsehood than to lose control by admitting truth? The Church has always accepted that it was to India that Jesus sent his apostle Thomas, and there are Christians in India today who claim descent from his converts. The Acts of Thomas are right as far as this is concerned; why should they not be right when they agree with the tradition that Jesus followed, and took his Mother with him?

It is not within the scope of this book nor the competence of its author to evaluate the evidence for Jesus's travels in the East: the books already mentioned can be consulted by whosoever needs to know what that evidence is. Here, it is enough to assert that though we do not know for certain much about the life of Jesus we do have reflected in the gospels the core of his teaching, and in the lives of those who have tried to follow that teaching, proof that what he taught was not just for the Jews of Roman Palestine but a doctrine that could guide and inspire all people of every age.

Mankind would be the poorer were it not so: and mankind has benefited from it, and will continue to do so, even though Jesus himself remains largely lost in the mists of time, ignored by many, resurrected by his latter-day disciples in a form of their own imagining.

Chapter VIII
Jesus: Teacher of Righteousness

Every individual who looks to the teaching of Jesus as a guide will see him in the image of their own creation. Those who belong to church organizations will have a picture of Jesus presented to them, on which their personal image will be largely based: but for all that the image will be personal.

Christianity survived because its legends and myths satisfied the needs of those for whom such beliefs were acceptable. The modern world, however, now knows too much. The only way that Jesus will be acceptable in the third millennium will be as a Teacher of Righteousness.

This will be the mark of the Christian of the future. Doubtless it will be argued that Christianity cannot be expected to survive as a world religion if, by the elimination of the popular myths and the invalidation of the authority of the gospels, Jesus Christ, its eponymous Founder, is reduced to a shadowy figure with little more to him than his name, too unsubstantial to attract the devotion of followers. That may at first appear the inevitable danger of too honest and thorough a reappraisal of our information about him.

It is undoubtedly true that much that the gospels record as words or deeds of Jesus cannot be taken as historically accurate: nevertheless, from the impression he clearly left on those who were closest to him there does emerge, through the myths of the past and the mists of time, an impression of a powerful and attractive personality – a Teacher of Righteousness – whose mission it was to teach the doctrine of the brotherhood of man and the fatherhood of God necessary for the present well-being of mankind and our future survival. If we start with the assumption that he was a man and not the incarnate Son of God, Jesus becomes not only more credible but also more admirable – a "man of God", indeed, but not beyond our comprehension: someone we can accept without prostituting our God-given intelligence or the dictates of reason.

Compared with other historically important figures of his period, and considering the world-wide influence of his name on history for nearly two thousand years, information about Jesus is sadly lacking. There is no contemporary record for most of his life, and the short period covered by the gospels is a record which is not only uncritical in its use of material but is sadly distorted by the bias of its authors. As it is, we know a great deal more about S.Paul and Pontius Pilate, and Herod the Great. To compose a portrait of him with no more to go on than what the New Testament tells us presents many problems. In the course of the last two thousand years and in our own time, the many attempts that have been made to portray Jesus in paintings, statues, on the stage and on the screen, have produced countless variations, each, to a large extent, influenced by the standards of the time and place in which they were made, and the theological beliefs of the portrayers. Unlike many of the personages of ancient history who achieved greatness or power in their own lifetime, Jesus was not commemorated by any contemporary statue or by having his head embossed on coins or medals.

The discovery in 1947 at Qumran, on the shores of the Dead Sea in Palestine, of the "Dead Sea Scrolls", gave hope that documents clearly referring to Christianity and even to Jesus might be found. Although since then further similar scrolls have been discovered and many of them are now available in translations, nothing new directly concerned with Jesus has come to light. Much has been revealed about the Essenes and their beliefs and aspirations, and the probable link between them and Jesus's life and teaching. New information may yet be uncovered. Unfortunately it has not been possible to establish with any certainty the exact date of individual scrolls, though it is believed most date from the first century B.C. Attempts have been made to associate Jesus with the Teacher of Righteousness mentioned in many of the Scrolls; but it has also seemed possible to associate him with The Wicked Priest, presented in some scrolls as the opposer of the Teacher of Righteousness. That a case may be made out for either identification greatly reduces the likelihood that either is correct. If we now call Jesus a Teacher of Righteousness it is not to identify him with the Teacher named in the scrolls, but rather as the fulfilment of the hope for such a teacher that the scrolls imply.

Although the scrolls may suggest something of the background to the teaching of Jesus, and the inspiration that prompted it, they seem, so far as they are at present known, to give us no information about his life or his person. They contain no text that is the origin of, or which has originated in, any of the gospel stories, although, as already mentioned, some of the hymns which appear in Luke may well have their origin in Essene hymns.

More valuable as a source of information on which to base our knowledge of what Jesus looked like is the Shroud of Turin. The Shroud has been studied and written about from at least 1581, but more particularly from the end of the last century onwards, since the discovery of photography made it possible to evaluate fully the negative image imprinted upon it. (A comprehensive bibliography can be found in *The Jesus Conspiracy* previously referred to.) For those who accept it as genuine it provides a 3-D photograph of Jesus as he was immediately after the crucifixion, a photograph not only of his face but of the whole body, back as well as front, showing the scars of the flagellation he received, the abrasions caused by the crown (or, rather, cap) of thorns, the wounds in wrists, feet and side. If genuine it is so exceptional a relic that in its preservation it would not be unreasonable to see the hand of divine Providence.

The body on the Shroud is that of a well-built man in the prime of life – someone capable of undertaking the arduous travelling that occupied so much of Jesus's time. The face is exactly what we would expect Jesus to have looked like, typically that of a Palestinian Jew, his hair and beard both in the style of the Nazarenes (or holy men) of his day. We have to assume that he would have had a fairly dark skin, a commanding yet calm and gentle expression, and deeply expressive eyes. With the features that are shown the face is completely convincing, as convincing as it is unlike any portrait of Jesus of medieval origin.

In Professor Hassnain's book, *A Search for the Historical Jesus*, there is a reproduction of the face on the Shroud, strikingly coloured by what appears to have been a modern miracle performed in Bangalore by an Indian religious teacher, Sathya Sai Baba, while holding an ordinary black and white photograph of the face of the Shroud. Sceptics must not dismiss as a fairy tale the account of how this was achieved until they have read for themselves the eye-witness account of what happened, and seen the coloured print. They may well discover that the printed reproduction, which still retains the marks of the creases on the Shroud, is, in itself, enough to compel belief.

Whatever their shortcomings as historical documents the gospels are sufficiently consistent in the way they portray Jesus to encourage us to believe that they reflect accurately enough the personality of Jesus as it appeared to those who knew him. If Jesus was as they portray him, his success as a teacher must have depended upon his having an imposing presence: without it he could not have made so great an impact on his audiences. Although at times he spoke in synagogues, normally he addressed large crowds in the open air, so his voice must have been powerful and his diction clear. In normal everyday situations he would have spoken Aramaic, his own mother tongue and the local language of the people of Palestine and of the Jewish colonies in the East. He was addressed as Rabbi, and was accepted as a man of some learning; as such he doubtless spoke Koine Greek, for Galilee was the most Hellenistic of the Palestinian provinces. As a student of the Scriptures and probably of some of the Essene writings he must have been able to read Hebrew. To these could have been added the knowledge of eastern languages acquired during his years in the East.

A source of information about the life of Jesus, which is generally ignored, although it has in fact been available for many years, is the large number of manuscripts mainly now preserved in Buddhist monasteries near the Kashmir and Tibet border. Some of these ancient Indian writings are, it is reported, actually in the Vatican library, but it would seem the Church authorities prefer to keep them hidden away. These Buddhist documents have not been subjected to the same minute and continuous scholarly scrutiny as have the New Testament texts; their dates are uncertain, the authority of their authorship unestablished. But they nevertheless form a very considerable weight of evidence for the claim that Jesus twice visited Kashmir and the Middle East countries and must have absorbed much of the teaching of Buddhism, by that time a well-established and widely-spread religion attaching much importance to the soul's development through ascetic living and meditation. He would inevitably have come into contact with Jainism, at that time already over five hundred years old. The Jains believe in improving the soul by living a pure life, and by kindness to others. They were vegetarians, as were most of the Essenes, and Jesus seems to have abstained from meat though not from fish. The Jains, though believing in the individual soul do not believe in a personal God – nor do Buddhists in the sense that Christians do: Jesus retained the Jewish belief in monotheism, but his God was not the wrathful despot of so much of the Hebrew Scriptures. In its most primitive form monotheism pictures the one Creator God much as the Greeks pictured Zeus – a super-human being, living somewhere above the earth, constantly interfering with it, driven by very human emotions of anger and ambition. Over the centuries the image has changed, and today those who still believe in a Creator God realize that he must be beyond human understanding, beyond our powers to describe him. But Jesus solved the difficulty by teaching that as far as we are concerned we should regard God as a Father, that is as our progenitor and the source of life and of all we need for it. The picture of God as a Father also implies that we are all siblings, all from earliest man to the last of the human race; in every age, in every corner of the world, whatever may be our ethnic differences. There are many today with somewhat kranky sexist ideas who want to call God "Mother": but the picture of him as Father does not imply gender – merely the idea of the ultimate source of being and the provider of all things. It was, in Jesus's days, an easily understood concept, and for those who are not diverted by side issues the picture of God as Father is conveniently valid today.

As a result of years of his contact with Buddhism, Jesus was a peace-loving missionary. But, just as he retained his Jewish monotheism, he seems also to have retained something of the fire of rebellion that stirred so many Galileans to revolt, although his revolt was not against Rome but against injustice and hypocrisy, against meaningless ritual and restrictive rules, and against those who put the Law of Moses above the laws of charity and mercy.

The gospels succeed in showing Jesus to have been essentially human: he showed all the characteristics of a normal man, with his strengths and his weaknesses. When circumstances so required he could be stern, even relentless. He did not hesitate to condemn sin and made it clear that unrepented wickedness would be punished. He was not afraid to show righteous anger or indignation, as when towards the end of his life, on his last visit to Jerusalem, he overturned the tables of the money-changers and the stools of the sellers of pigeons who had set up shop in the Temple precinct, desecrating "his Father's house" – an attitude of mind consistent with someone with an Essene-style outlook on religion (Mtt 21,22ff – told by the other gospels also, but John 2.13ff puts it earlier). And when it came to his own disciples, men mainly of the same self-employed and independent artisan class as himself, he could be equally stern where necessary: he was not slow to rebuke them when they did not come up to scratch. He doubtless knew, even if they didn't, that later, when he would need to send them out to further his teaching, often among hostile crowds, they would have to face much worse dangers and discomforts, and they would need both courage and perseverance to a far greater degree than that needed during their discipleship. He warned those who thought they could follow in his footsteps as an ascetic to be ready, if necessary, to abandoned all worldly goods, even family attachments. Yet in spite of his personal gifts, his strength of mind and body acquired through long years of travel, ascetic living and spiritual training, the gospels portray him as a normal approachable being, aware of his own limitations, enjoying the companionship of those he loved best, Mary Magdalen and his disciple John; and though he may have rebuked his mother he continued to show her filial duty and affection. Like all of us, he had an instinctive fear of pain and death – that powerful instinct necessary for the survival of our species. Jesus was no exception: he felt fear and he suffered pain. Doubtless, too, he felt the same instinctive temptations that beset us all, including those of lust and greed – his understanding of those who suffered and were conquered by them suggests as much. The descriptions of his "Temptation in the Desert", as given by Matthew (4,1-22) and Luke (4,1-23), even if not to be taken literally, drive this point home. He was, from what the gospels tell us, "every inch a man". Perhaps as a result of time spent in a Buddhist monastic environment together with much journeying on foot in the mountainous area of Kashmir, Jesus was more able than most to face considerable physical strain and discomfort, and to live very frugally. But he did not make a show of doing so: when he was offered hospitality he was always glad to accept it, always ready to accept gracefully any consideration or comfort his hosts wished to offer him. Jesus was not narrow-minded. He did not lack compassion and understanding of human foibles and weaknesses. He was always ready to listen to those who had troubles, especially to the sick and social outcasts, seeking to cure the former, welcoming the latter, whoever they might be, whether Jews, despised inhabitants of Samaria, or hated Romans. He was not afraid to act when he thought it right to do so – he was what we might call today "his own man".

It has been said that Jesus was less than human because he is never reported to have laughed. But of how many personalities of the ancient world, whose lives have been recorded, are we told that they laughed? The evangelists recorded his mission from such material as was available to them; they did not attempt to describe his character, and they hardly mention what he did when not actively engaged on his main task. But we are told that Jesus wept (John, 11,35), and (as we have seen) he could exhibit anger and affection: he was a man who was not afraid to show his feelings, and who can doubt that such a man could also laugh? He was fond of children – how could he have gathered them around him unless he smiled? and he who smiles also laughs when the occasion arises. Jesus was not so ostentatiously ascetic as to refuse to share in the social life of his friends, and in so doing he must have shared their laughter. And it is not possible that he could have attracted such large crowds as those that gathered eagerly to hear him speak if his preaching had not been spiced with humour. After a long day of teaching, as Jesus and his closest companions made their tired way to wherever they would eat and sleep they doubtless discussed, and, with Jesus, chuckled over, the events of the day as they recalled not only the woes of the sick and the sinners, but the little human comedies that had lightened their day. We don't know – but it is impossible to believe that a man of so many parts and so well adjusted did not laugh.

Though gentle with the poor and sick, Jesus stood up to Pontius Pilate, the Roman Procurator in Jerusalem, when he was accused by the Chief Priests of being a danger to the imperial power of Rome. He faced him with dignity and without animosity, and, as all four gospels agree albeit in slightly different words, Pilate failed to find fault with him (Mtt, 27,26; Mk,115,24; Lk, 23,4; Jn,18,38). There is no mention of Jesus having written anything. He most certainly could have done so, and perhaps he did. But no one has suggested that he wrote anything in the form of a record of his teaching. Had he done so it is difficult to believe it would not have been most carefully preserved, and inevitably there would have been forgeries claiming to be his work. That he did not do so may have been deliberate. It is probable that Jesus, like Buddha, but unlike other great religious teachers such as Mohammed, who dictated the Koran during his lifetime for the instruction of his followers, foresaw the problems that would arise if he had done so. Had he written, he would have probably chosen to write in Hebrew, the "literary" language of the Jews, rather than in his own native Aramaic or the widely used Koine Greek of the time. He would have been confined in what he wrote to ideas that could be expressed and understood at that time. He could not, for example, have laid down laws about the use of nuclear weapons, the duties of trade unions, or the rights and wrongs of *in vitro* fertilization. Such things were unknown; the words for them did not exist, the problems they present had not been thought of and would have meant nothing at the time. He could have written only what was relevant to the problems of the world in which he lived. Even the translation of whichever language he might have chosen would have given rise to disputes about his meaning due to the changes that occur in any language when used over many centuries. A "code of belief and conduct", on the interpretation of which no one agrees, can prove a poor authority by which to live.

There is every indication that Jesus did not marry before the crucifixion. If an Essene, he probably took a vow of celibacy. The Essene vow of celibacy was not necessarily taken for life, but in Jesus's case would doubtless have been intended for the period of his teaching. During his years of preparation marriage would have been impossible, and he remained a Nazarene, a "holy man" to the end of his mission. Living among Buddhists as a holy man (as their records suggest), while still in India, Jesus might well have already adopted celibacy for life. He was still reputed the "Nazarene" (*ho Nazdoraios*, John,19,19) at the time of his crucifixion. Most English versions of this verse translate this to mean "of Nazareth", but this is incorrect. John uses the Greek *apo Nazdaret* for "from Nazareth" (John,1,45), and thus the Greek words for Nazarene and for Nazareth are clearly quite distinct. Nevertheless, as is characteristic of the truly religiously dedicated celibate, Jesus certainly respected and upheld the dignity of the married state. Towards women he was tolerant of those who went astray and appreciative of those who showed affection. It has already been mentioned how, when he was sure that he was dying, he gave a special thought to the future care of his Mother, and if the Indian tradition is correct took her with him on his return to Kashmir.

To what extent Jesus reflected in his teaching the views of the Essenes is not easy to ascertain since the varied groups who were classed as Essenes were probably separate sects with somewhat differing doctrines, practices and aims, some more pacific, some more militant; than others. But his rescue from the tomb, if indeed Essene inspired and Essene organized, must mean he remained to the end high in their esteem – however much he may have preached and lived according to his own vision of God's kingdom. He could not have differed materially from the beliefs and aspirations of his sponsors. To say, therefore, that he was himself an Essene may be true if the term is used in its broadest sense, somewhat in the same way as "nonconformist" can be applied to many different but similar Christian groups today. There is every indication from Acts (2,43), and from what we know of their life-style, that what inspired the earliest Christians who gathered together under S.James in Jerusalem, was the Essene-like teaching of Jesus, not the salvation theology of S.Paul, and for this reason they, too, were known as

"Nazarenes".

There are, in the gospels, passages which clearly indicate belief in Jesus's being more than an ordinary man. The most obvious of these is the story of the event called "The Transfiguration" (Mtt,17,1; Mk,9,2: Lk,9,28). According to Mark, Jesus took SS.Peter, James and John up into a mountain, where before their eyes his clothes became shining white, and they saw Elijah and Moses speaking with Jesus, and S.Peter offered to make them three tents. And a voice was heard saying: "This is my dear Son; listen to him!" And then looking round they saw only Jesus. Matthew gives the same story with a little more detail. Luke includes the information that Moses and Elijah talked with Jesus about how he would soon fulfil God's purpose by dying in Jerusalem – this while S.Peter and his companions were asleep; they awoke to see Jesus's glory and the two men. The voice from a cloud said: "This is my Son whom I have chosen – listen to him!" It seems strange that John does not also include an event which is so much in tune with its *Logos* Prologue, especially if the S.John of the Transfiguration is the John who inspired the gospel that bears his name. The story fits unnaturally into the synoptics, so much so that one cannot help feeling that it was inserted from some late source, common to all three, at a time when the doctrine of the Incarnation was beginning to become part of the Church's official doctrine; this would have been after the completion of John which could explain why the story does not appear in it.

The way in which Jesus was perceived underwent various stages of evolution, from the years immediately following the crucifixion, to when the synoptics were being written and added to, and on into the first decade of the second century. The sect known as the Ebionites seem to have represented the view of the very first Christians, those who gathered round S. James in Jerusalem soon after the crucifixion. They were Jews, obedient to the Law of Moses, who were disciples of Jesus but who did not believe in his divinity, but only that he was a divinely inspired teacher. They were opposed to S.Paul's teaching; but his teaching, and the philosophy of Philo Judaeus of Alexandria, became the generally accepted theology and philosophy, and the Ebionites were declared heretics. The *Logos* (the Word) in the Prologue with which John begins, which in Philo's philosophy stood for "that by which God expressed himself" was further developed by S.Paul, and evolved into the idea that Jesus was not merely "that by which God expresses himself" but God himself incarnate. In the course of time this became the Church's official teaching. The story of the Transfiguration may well be an example of how a simple account of a secret encounter which Jesus had with two of his Essene masters was given the form in which it appears in the synoptics to emphasize the newly-evolved doctrine of the Incarnation then in vogue – one more example (like the birth stories) of the text of the gospels being doctored to fit the accepted teaching rather than fitting the teaching to the text. Fortunately, as we have seen, if we probe back into the origins of the legends about Jesus and discard the obvious myths there remains sufficient to recall a balanced portrait of the man, and the substance of his message for mankind.

It is ironic that although it was due to S.Paul that the true image of Jesus and his mission were obscured by the apostle's own doctrine, it is almost certainly due to that doctrine that any knowledge of the true Jesus and his teaching has survived. S.Paul's teaching gave hope to those who had little to hope for; he laid the foundations for a religion that would be attractive enough for martyrs to die for, a religion that fitted well into the social and political structure of western civilization of his own time and that of the centuries that were to follow; a religion that fitted so well within the limited range of medieval knowledge. Through the survival of S.Paul's salvation theology the gospels were preserved and with them the teaching of Jesus: a teaching which although it offers little in the way of dogmatic theology has proved a never-failing inspiration for those seeking spiritual advancement and moral guidance. The dogmatic theology in which the message of Jesus has been encased, and almost extinguished, has not been able to withstand the onslaught of man's progress in knowledge of the world about him; and like the outgrown skin of a snake is now being sloughed off. Although we may never know more about Jesus Christ himself, his teaching thus freed may yet survive, and as the Christianity of the third millennium more worthily mirror the mind of him whose name it bears.

Jesus's Family Tree

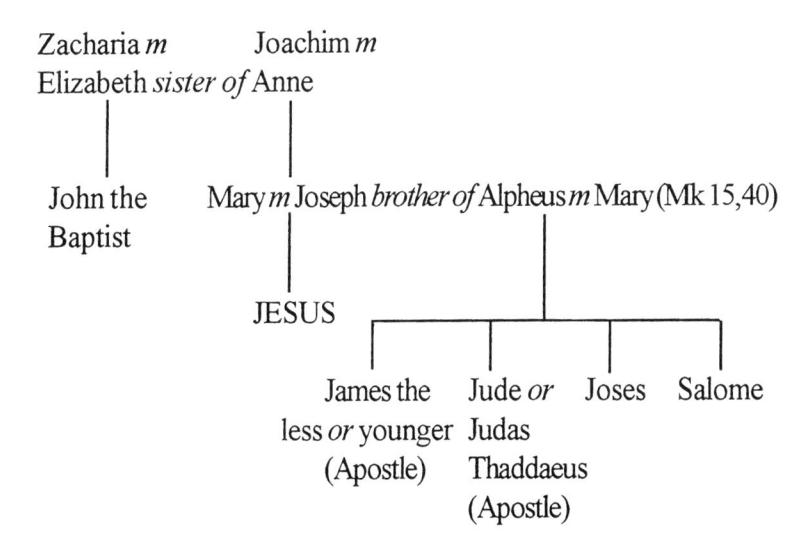

Zacharia *m*   Joachim *m*
Elizabeth *sister of* Anne

John the Baptist   Mary *m* Joseph *brother of* Alpheus *m* Mary (Mk 15,40)

JESUS

- James the less *or* younger (Apostle)
- Jude *or* Judas Thaddaeus (Apostle)
- Joses
- Salome

James the Less or James the Younger is called by S.Paul "the brother of the Lord" (Galatians,1,18) but he was in fact a first cousin. He became first "bishop" of Jerusalem, and was martyred. His mother was not the same Mary as the mother of Jesus.

CHAPTER IX
THE CHURCH IN THE THIRD MILLENNIUM

The great error of the past was to make the Church the guardian of a creed, with the result that it became enslaved by the bonds of its own dogma. Jesus did not found a Church. He could not have foreseen, indeed he could not have imagined, the organization that was to evolve in his name about a hundred years after his birth. As a man of his own time, he presented his message as befitted the world in which he lived.

The Greek word in the New Testament translated by "church" in English versions is *ekkleesia*, which means a gathering of those called together. In this sense it is used frequently in both Acts and the Epistles, and came in time to mean the organization that controlled gatherings of believers – first as local "Churches", then their union into one centralized body. Some groups of local Churches did not accept its authority and were considered heretical sects. The main body, formed from those who accepted the theology of Paul, being the strongest became The Church. As "The One True Church" it retained its unity for a while until in due course the eastern and western sections split, the eastern forming the Eastern Orthodox Church, now mainly represented by the Russian and Greek Orthodox Churches, the western forming the Roman Catholic Church. This, in its turn, finally lost its unity at the time of the Reformation with the formation of Protestant Churches and sects.

The word "church" is only twice reported to have been used by Jesus himself, both in Matthew. On the second of these occasions Jesus was clearly referring to a religious gathering: speaking of the way to treat a sinful brother he said: "tell all to the church ..." (Matthew,18,15-17). The other, earlier, occasion was when he is reported to have made the well-known statement "You are Peter, a rock, and on this rock I shall build my church" (Matthew,16,18).

On this statement is largely based the claims of the Papacy and the Roman Church. But it is obvious that the passage must be a later interpolation. Clearly, the use of a word meaning "church" in the sense of the organized Church that was to evolve after his death would have meant nothing to Jesus or to his disciples at the time these words were supposed to have been spoken. They only acquired such a meaning some seventy or more years later when the early Church was becoming an organized body. It was then, and not till then, that the statement became important: those representing the newly emerging church organization wanted to prove its legitimacy by claiming its authority had been derived from Peter, the chosen head of the apostles.

"The Church", when used here in a general sense, includes all the major recognized Christian Churches – the Roman Catholic, eastern Orthodox, the world-wide Anglican Communion, the Presbyterians, Methodists and Baptists. All these Churches have inherited the basic doctrines of the theology of Paul. Each of these exerts considerable influence in different parts of the world, and each is the dominant form of Christianity in one or another country. In England (but not in the whole United Kingdom) there still remains an officially recognized "state" Church – the Church of England – with the reigning Monarch as head of both the religious and the secular national authority. It is for this reason that the Church of England is so broad in its acceptance of a wide range of views, many of them theologically very different: it has to be broad enough to accommodate Christians of a great variety of traditions, those of the most vague and those of the most dogmatic persuasions. It is also for this reason that, whatever may happen elsewhere, the Church of England is ideally suited to survive the effects of such reappraisals of the teaching about Jesus, his person, his life, and his message, such as that attempted in this book. Unless the Church of England – and, indeed, all Christian institutions – are prepared to face up to the facts revealed by modern scientific and historical investigation, they will become atrophied, replaced by the freakish and irrational substitutes which already attract all too easily the ill-informed and easily swayed – or succumb to the apparent attractions of Islam or Buddhism, leaving the nation bereft of moral and spiritual guidance, robbing it of its Christian heritage. It is a choice between Christianity brought up to date or chaos. Although Jesus did not found a "Church", as the result of his teaching, he did initiate a Movement – and, unlike the Church which has become trapped by its own dogma, a movement implies development, progress, evolution. Fortunately, in spite of the unrealistic philosophical theories that through two thousand years have masqueraded as "Christianity", much of the mind of Jesus has survived, in spite of the trappings of Pauline theology which have all but obscured it. The example of Jesus's life and the underlying ethos of his teaching have been the inspiration for countless Christian lives down through the centuries; the spiritual and ethical truths of real "Christianity", the essential characteristics of the message of Jesus, have, as it were, been cocooned in the silken thread of dogma and myth, providentially woven about it for their preservation.

We are entering the third millennium, and an age of discovery of many new unsuspected secrets of nature is opening out before us. It may take another thousand years for our knowledge to reach the potential limits of our understanding – limits which, perhaps may never be reached – but dawn has broken and light is spreading through the minds of those who are not too timid to open their eyes to see and their minds to understand. When the lingering outdated medieval doctrines are finally discarded and the inhibitions that thwart open research abandoned, it may prove possible to put Jesus in his rightful place – in the foremost rank of great religious teachers. Removing the myths of dogmatic Christianity does not reduce Jesus to a minor itinerant Palestinian preacher – it enables him to be recognized for what he really was, a Teacher of world dimensions, in whose title of "Christ" – the Anointed One – his followers will be proud to share by calling themselves Christians, members of the Church of Christ.

Although misrepresented, but fortunately also preserved within the framework of Pauline theology, much of the teaching of Jesus has already become part of the universal *mores* of the human race; now widely taken for granted, its effects having spread beyond official Christendom to become absorbed into the ethics both of those who have other faiths as well as of those with none. That we are all children of one God is now widely accepted by those who believe in God – that we are all members of one *genus homo* is accepted by both those who believe in God and those who do not. We all share the same genes, we all share the same speck of dust in the universe which is our world; we all have a brief loan of the priceless treasure – life: we all share the same mortality. In his parables, in the "Sermon on the Mount", and in the "Lord's Prayer" – those elements of his teaching that reflect the core of his teaching and which are most widely known – Jesus taught how we should serve God as children of a common Father, and how we can live together in dignity and harmony, recognizing the sanctity of the life of every individual, our inviolable fraternal heritage, each one of us equally precious in the sight of God (Matthew, 18, 10-14).

It may seem absurd to imagine that institutional Christianity as presented by the major Churches can possibly undergo the changes that modern knowledge requires of it, and survive in anything like its present form. The idea is not as absurd as it first appears. The ecumenical movement, though still in its early stages, recognizes that it is essentially the teaching of Jesus, not formulated dogmas, that must unite his followers into one united, if diversified, Church.

It has already been suggested that many of those who profess to hold traditional orthodox beliefs no longer do so in the secret of their hearts. Of necessity, perhaps, what ceases to be tenable is quietly swept under the carpet, eventually to be forgotten. An example of how such changes occur is the doctrine that was once universally accepted as fundamental to Christian teaching: that death came into the world through sin – through the original sin of Adam – that God created man with the intent that he should be immortal – not just in his soul but in the complete person, body and soul together. Such a doctrine could only have originated at a time when the theory of Evolution and the laws governing all animal life were unknown, and the world's limited capacity and lifetime were ignored. It remains part of the official teaching of much of orthodox Christendom – but how many professing Christians really believe that the mortality of the body is due to anything but natural processes? how many believe that man's sexual appetites are anything other than an instinct inherited from our sub-human ancestors to ensure the survival of our species, not given by God that we may increase and multiply? Such an attitude towards sex could only have been conceived when the limitations of the earth's resources were not a matter of concern, when the possibility of the earth becoming over-populated was unthinkable.

Traditional teaching about hell, of which Christians were once so vividly reminded by the imaginative artistry of the west windows of medieval churches, presented a God of infinite cruelty towards those whose human weaknesses had led them astray – condemning them to mental and physical torture for eternity – unjustly, if Paul's doctrine of the one sufficient sacrifice of the Incarnate Son is taken into consideration. Modern theology has been forced by the virtual rejection of such teaching to modify the picture of the torture-flames of hell, and of the pains of purgatory, in which earlier centuries appear to have taken a gruesome delight; but many such doctrines remain a part of the official teaching professed unwittingly by millions through their membership of the Church to which they belong.

Discarding the chains of outworn dogmas and clearing away the cobwebs of myth does not mean discarding all the treasures that the past has produced. The organized Churches are man-made institutions; they were created to satisfy the needs of their members at the time in which they came into being, adopting the structures that reflected the society in which they evolved. If they are to remain living entities and not survive as mere stagnant monuments to the past they must continue to evolve, continue to serve the needs of each passing age. Just as at the Reformation the Protestant Churches adapted to the new modes of thought of the time, so now, as new light is shed on the past, they must not fear to reassess the Christian message, and re-express the old in terms that befit the new: enriched by what has been, enlightened by what is yet to come.

For the individual who has been brought up to believe in traditional Christianity and for whom its acceptance has been a matter of course, to break away from convictions firmly held for many years, from the teaching of childhood, will not be easy. Lifelong religious practices and assumptions can so condition the mind that even when faced with concrete evidence to the contrary there will always be those unable to accept that they have been living in a world of make-believe. At times a sub-conscious fear may blind the mind to new truths; it may appear a virtue, a sacred duty, to repulse such truths as the work of the devil. Some there will be who will not be able to abandon what they hold dear, and old beliefs will linger on: but with each generation the hold of the past will inevitably dwindle as evolving truth becomes more and more irresistible.

For those who speak for the Church it is different. It is the duty of those who are its pastors to face boldly what they may already inwardly and only with reluctance recognize as the truth. It must surely be wrong not to look at the evidence as it is revealed, wrong to continue to teach others as if such evidence did not exist. Both the present strength and future survival of their Church depends on its representatives being prepared to recognize that truth continues to unfold. It should be a matter of rejoicing, not (as some doubtless regard it) one for alarm, that the Church of England already leads the way in this wider conception of what it means to be a Christian.

Truth cannot be manufactured to match preconceptions; it cannot be hidden or ignored for ever, though it would seem there are still some who won't face this fact. The information about Jesus's probable years in India has been known for a hundred years; yet books teaching apologetics and theology, books that claim to describe all we know of his life, seem only too eager to ignore it. Because the early Church limited the available information about Jesus to the contents of the four gospels, other writings which might have shed more light on his life and teaching became forbidden reading, many were destroyed. There has been a conspiracy of silence which has caused incalculable damage to the truth about Jesus which it is high time Church leaders recognized and endeavoured to repair. No one should imagine that, considered from a purely practical standpoint, it is an easy matter for a leading cleric inwardly to admit that he can no longer with integrity accept tenets of his faith that he knows are patently flawed. If he openly questions the creed he is supposed to promote, he loses his position and with it his teaching authority. Yet it is the position he holds that gives him the authority to teach, and the duty to teach truth as he sees it. If he lives a lie he retains his authority and abuses it; if he uses his authority to show how the Church he represents has erred in the past and must restate truth in more acceptable terms, the very authority by which he speaks may well be lost. But the future of Christianity and the future of his Church depend on his retaining his position and working within the Church to ease it out of the past into the future. This is the dilemma that must face all those who feel themselves called to what is generally called "the ministry". It is a dilemma that calls for the wisdom of Solomon to resolve. In England, in spite of the presence of many other religious minorities – indeed, because of them – we need our national Church – the Church of England. It has an essential role to play in the life of a nation that calls itself "Christian". To fulfil such a task the Church of England, in England, is ideally placed to fulfil the task, and in doing so act as an example for "less happier lands". It can provide a channel for enlightenment through those dedicated to its service; it already has the practical organization and its material presentation ready to hand, through the accident of history, the inheritance of its past.

For the majority of human beings, gathering together in fellowship is a natural instinct, whether to share a danger or express a common act of worship. The worship may be for some primitive tribal god, an idealized sportsman or pop group, or God himself. The need to worship God, whether or not rationally inspired, is usually more permanent than the temporary enthusiasms of youthful fancy, and normally it is one that needs to be shared with others. It is a need common to all races, and to all times – one that may call for constant and regular expression as a part of life, or one that is felt only at moments of sorrow, hope or joy. There are occasions in most lives when the individual wants to feel a part of something greater than himself, to share with others the same emotions, aspirations, convictions. The Church has in the past provided the means to satisfy such needs at their highest, most spiritual level, and it must continue to do so.

The material legacy of the past, the actual buildings, chapels, churches and cathedrals, still have their part to play. They are more than mere monuments to the faith of our ancestors: they offer the pilgrim soul sanctuary from the turbulence of worldly interests, and enrich the fruits of the future with the prayers and worship of the past. They are a constant reminder in our midst that there is a spiritual element in life, and other values not measured by material success.

The forms of worship as practised in the past have evolved as the natural expression of human nature. The use of the psalms and hymns dates back to long before Jesus's days; they formed part of the worship familiar to him and his earliest followers; their continued use links all generations together – present Christians with those of every earlier age, with the first disciples of Jesus, and with Jesus himself. The traditional offices of Matins and Evensong, Compline and Vespers, are rewarding forms of community worship which have little to do with outmoded doctrines. In the past the Church has absorbed into its calendar popular elements of pagan religions; it can equally well retain elements of medieval mythology as symbolic expressions of truths beyond our understanding. Gregorian plainsong and, in England, Tudor choral music, can still provide inspiration and food for the soul; the major traditional Christian festivals, the well-loved rites and rituals, the symbolism of vestments and furnishings, must not be thrown away – they remain a treasury of the spiritual values that inspired them. Because Jesus did not die on the Cross does not mean it ceases to be the symbol par excellence of Christianity. The Cross was the ultimate sermon of his life – that the supreme virtue is submission to the will of God at whatever cost; it also symbolizes the victory of Jesus over those who attempted to use the Cross to prevent his message being given to the world. As things turned out, it had the opposite effect. It gave the message of Jesus the impetus that ensured its survival.

Among all the treasures of medieval Christianity the religious orders must rank very highly. Through them learning was kept alight in a dark age, art and music and medicine were all enriched and advanced. Today those who teach, who care for the sick, the poor, the aged, are all carrying on traditions founded on the teachings of Jesus, on reality, not on myth. Of less obvious importance, but close to the prayer and contemplation that played so large a part in his life, are the contemplative orders, especially the Benedictines. The Rule of S.Benedict (about AD529) has continued to be followed virtually unchanged down to the present day, and has proved so successful because it provides in so moderate a form the possibility for those ordinary men and women who feel called to do so to live a life of prayer and the search for God – a calling that was already held in high esteem by the wisdom of the East long before it helped mould the mind of Jesus. The Rule is kindly and tolerant, yet reflects the mode of life of the ascetic Nazarene. It survives today because it still answers to a need; the exceptionally well balanced person that is the typical Benedictine is evidence enough that monastic life is not an anachronism: such spiritual centres are needed in any society to balance the downward pull of materialism. S.Paul was not wrong in everything, and he was very right when he compared the different individuals who together make up the Church with the different parts of the human body, each with its own special function (1 Corinthians, 12,14ff). The contemplative monasteries of monks and nuns are like the "glands" that, silently and secretly, manufacture and release into the bloodstream chemicals essentials to the working of the body. Their function may appear less obvious than that of the eye or the hand: but for very life itself they are vital.

The baptism of children, marriages, burials, dedications, thanksgivings – these are important events in the life of individuals and families; some religious organization that can highlight their importance will always be necessary. They provide salutary moments of recollection for those absorbed by otherwise materially orientated lives.

Great state occasions, coronations, moments of national peril, rejoicings or commemorations, all call for some form of ceremonial solemnity – and the need for the dignity of a religious service in a building dedicated to such occasions is a natural need in the life of any nation: it has always been so, and so it will always be. As long as the necessary organization – the Church – remains for such occasions, so too will there always be those who feel themselves called to act as its ministers. Human beings vary widely in the way in which they picture themselves, in their self-esteem and in the manner they seek fulfilment, and the idea that a "vocation" is a call from God may be an illusion; but if the illusion results in making the most of one's natural talents and inclinations for the benefit of others, then it is no bad thing. It is part of the function of a Church to nurture such ambitions and to direct towards the general good the efforts of those who wish to serve – to direct, instruct – restrain, perhaps – but not enslave.

As a nation, we need a Church as the guardian of our ethics and as a bulwark against fanaticism. We need a Church to teach and help us to maintain our understanding of what is right and what is wrong; what are the true values of life beyond considerations of pounds and pence. We need a Church that can recognize and direct the call of service to others, of giving as well as taking, a Church to enrich life with meaning and fulfilment, and, for those who accept the leadership of Jesus, the assurance that our passage in this world is something more than a flash of consciousness in an eternity of oblivion.

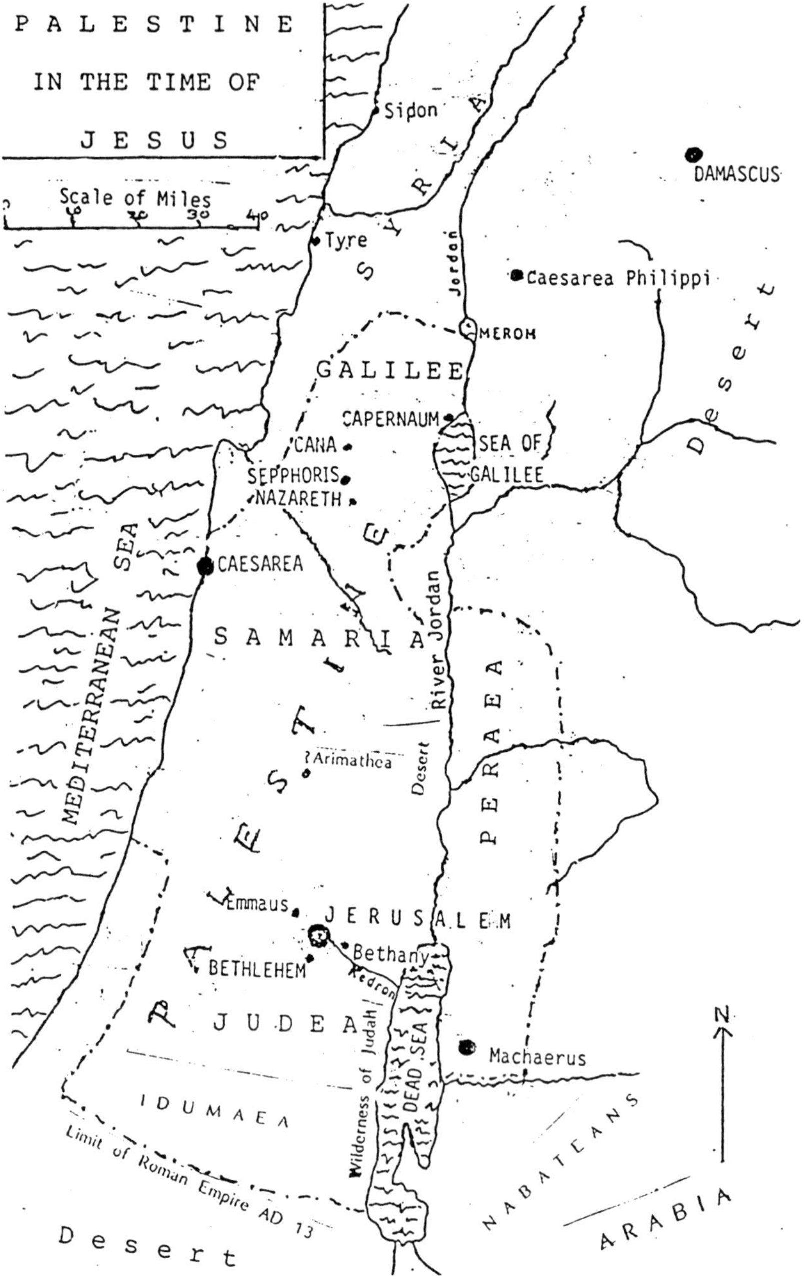
PALESTINE
IN THE TIME OF
JESUS
Scale of Miles
10 20 30 40
Sidon
SYRIA
DAMASCUS
Tyre
Jordan
Caesarea Philippi
Desert
MEROM
GALILEE
CAPERNAUM
SEA OF
GALILEE
CANA
SEPPHORIS
NAZARETH
MEDITERRANEAN SEA
CAESAREA
SAMARIA
River Jordan
PALESTINE
PERAEA
?Arimathea
Desert
Emmaus
JERUSALEM
Bethany
BETHLEHEM
Kedron
JUDEA
Wilderness of Judah
DEAD SEA
Machaerus
N
IDUMAEA
Limit of Roman Empire AD 13
NABATEANS
ARABIA
Desert

APPENDIX
FOR RAPID REFERENCE
1
Persons Places and Subjects

The following Alphabetical list should enable the reader to check persons, places and terms appearing in the text when the need arises.

A List of Dates follows; this should also be useful for rapid reference.

Abraham: founder of the Hebrew people (the Israelites or Jews). Lived at some time about two thousand or more years BC – that is, some four thousand years ago. Burial place unknown.

Agrippa I: grandson of Herod the Great. Born 11BC, and was for a while Tetrarch of Galilee and Peraea after the banishment of Antipas (below). Assassinated in AD44 by Simon Magus.

Agrippa II: son of Agrippa I. Born AD27, but did not become king until AD47 as too young when his father died. Appointed to rule Galilee by Nero in AD54. Was much influenced by S.Paul. Died AD100.

Alexandria: capital city of Egypt at the time of Jesus and important port. It had an early group of Christians, said to have been founded by S.Mark. Renowned for an extensive library and for its school of medicine. There was also an Essene community there, renowned for healing skills, known as the theraputae. Buddhist missionaries had settled there some two hundred years before the birth of Jesus.

Angel: a spiritual Being who acts as a messenger – the word means "messenger". In art, angels are depicted as superior human-like beings with wings. In the gospels they are used as the means of conveying God's messages. It seems possible that the "angels" mentioned in the gospels were, in fact, representatives of the leaders of the Essenes who wore white garments.

Antipas: son of Herod the Great. Tetrach (administrator) of Galilee and Peraea AD4-39. Was responsible for the death of John the Baptist, who criticized his putting away his first wife, daughter of Aretas (below) and replacing her with his half-niece Herodias who was already married to another of her uncles. Antipas was in Jerusalem at the time of the crucifixion of Jesus. Was finally banished to Lyons (Roman "Lugdunum") and died AD39.

Archelaus: son of Herod the Great. On the death of his father became Tetrarch (administrator) of Judea but was dismissed in AD6, and died in exile AD14. He was even more unpleasant than his father. See Judea below.

Apostle: eleven of the "disciples" (see below) of Jesus were selected after his death to carry on his work. They were called "apostles", the word coming from a Greek word meaning "sent out". There were also three other apostles, not numbered among the twelve disciples, among them the most famous of all, S.Paul (see Paul, below).

Aretas IV: an Arabian king of the Nabateans, to the east of Palestine, whose daughter was the first wife of Antipas (above). To revenge his daughter when she was put away by Herod the Great he attacked Peraea, a province ruled by Antipas, and defeated him but was then in his turn punished by a Roman army from Syria, in AD37. Reigned 9BC to AD40.

Bethlehem: the small town a little over five miles south of Jerusalem, where Jesus was born, but not his home town (see Nazareth). It was associated with David (see below), and the old Jewish prophecies foretold that it would be the birthplace of the Messiah (see below)

Bible: the sacred or holy book of Christians. It is in two parts. See "Old Testament" and "New Testament" below.

Canon: with reference to the books of the Bible the "canon" is those books recognized by the Church as part of the divinely inspired Holy Scripture. The canon of the New Testament was finally settled in AD397 at the Council of Carthage.

Caiaphas: Joseph Caiaphas was the High Priest of the Temple in Jerusalem from about AD16 to AD36. As High Priest he was responsible to the Romans for law and order in and around Jerusalem. In this the Romans made use of the accepted custom of Jews.

Christianity: the religion of those who belong to the religion nominally founded by Jesus Christ, although in practice much of the doctrine of traditional orthodox Christianity as it finally evolved is due to the teaching of S.Paul. A "Christian" is one whose religion is Christianity, although the word is sometimes used loosely for persons who behave well. (See "Jesus Christ".)

Church: this word is used in two ways. The buildings where Christians go for worship are usually called churches, though smaller buildings, and those attached to institutions such as schools, colleges, hospitals, etc., are usually called chapels, as are many places of worship of some more modern sects. Very large churches which are the chief church in an area headed by a bishop are called cathedrals; and a few other large churches are called basilicas. The word "Church" is also used to describe a large organized group of Christians. Of these the Roman Catholic Church, claiming some 600 million members, is the largest, spread throughout the world. In England the national church, of which the Queen is the Head, is called The Church of England, and most of the older church buildings in England belong to the Church of England. There are numerous other "churches" – organized groups of Christians – in the British Isles. The term "the Church" used in these pages refers to the combined bodies of organized Christians.

Crucifixion: a cruel form of execution used by the Romans. Chapter VII, describing the crucifixion of Jesus, gives details.

David: lived about 1,000 years before Jesus. Considered the greatest of the Kings of Israel (that is, of the Jewish people). It was in Bethlehem that David was anointed King. He knit the twelve tribes of Israel into one nation and established Jerusalem as the capital city of the Jews.

Dead Sea Scrolls: manuscripts, many of them fragmentary, mainly in Hebrew or Aramaic, found in caves near the north west coast of the Dead Sea, the first being discovered in 1947. Probably written over a period from approximately 250BC to AD70. Written by as many as five hundred different hands. The assumption that they came from the nearby Qumran does not seem to be correct: they were more likely to have been from Jerusalem, removed to the caves for safety during the AD66-70 uprising against the Romans. Some have been translated into English and are available in bookshops. Much work is still to be done as many MSS have to be reassembled from minute fragments. Some at least are of Essene origin, perhaps from various Essene communities including that in Jerusalem.

Diaspora: when applied to the Jews, refers to the Jewish communities in exile: those scattered around the eastern Mediterranean lands, known as the Diaspora of the Greeks, and those in Syria, Persia, Mesopotamia, India, etc., known as the Aramaic Diaspora from the language they used.

Disciple: in general a "disciple" is someone who follows a certain teaching, and is not necessarily connected with religion. But in this book the word is used in two ways: any follower of the teachings of Jesus and, where the context so indicates, any of the men specially chosen by Jesus as followers who, all but one, later became "apostles". The exception, Judas Iscariot, became a traitor (see Judas Iscariot, below).

Ephesus: former ancient important city on the coast of Asia Minor, about the same latitude as Athens across the Aegean Sea. Frequently visited by S.Paul. Traditionally the last home of S.John, apostle and evangelist, and place where the fourth gospel was possibly written.

Essenes: the name given to a religious sect or movement, of the Jews dating from at least 150BC up to the time of the destruction of Jerusalem in AD70. (See Nazarenes, below). The term "Essene" was used by the Roman historian Pliny, writing about AD75 to describe a "tribe" of Jews living in a celibate community, without women, on the west coast of the Dead Sea, but there is no evidence that Qumran housed such a community (see Qumran). The Jewish philosopher Philo (see below), who was born in Alexandria about 15BC, says the Essenes did not eat meat (but some of them certainly did), and did not practice animal sacrifices. He suggested the origin of the word "Essene" was the Greek "*Osseeotes*", meaning "the holy ones". For those Essenes who did not normally eat meat their Passover meal consisted of unleavened bread instead of the traditional lamb. There was an Essene community in Alexandria at that time when Philo wrote, and his description may have been correct, as far as they were concerned, without necessarily applying to all the reforming sects to whom the title was later applied. Josephus (see below), writing about AD85, described them as a Jewish sect living strict celibate lives, but with a "second order" who did marry. They were well versed in the Scriptures and were strict adherents to the Law of Moses. In general, contemporary writers seem to have used the term "Essene" loosely to denote Jews endeavouring to live what they considered was a purer form of Judaism. The Essenes did not themselves use the term. The monastic Essenes lived mainly celibate lives in communities and the "lay" Essenes lived normal, but strictly religious, lives.

Eusebius: born in Palestine. c.AD264-349. Became bishop of Caesarea. c.313. Important as church historian who quoted from earlier writers (e.g. Papias) whose own works have since been lost.

Evangelist: there are only four evangelists in the sense used in this book. They are the four authors of the four gospels (see below). Traditionally they are S.Matthew, S.Mark, S.Luke and S.John. The first and last of these became apostles; the other two worked with apostles. Whether these four men actually wrote the books attributed to them is discussed in Chapter IV.

Gabriel: the traditional name of one of the most important of the angels, sent by God on special missions. Only two other angels are given names in the Bible: Michael and Raphael. Mentioned also as God's messenger in the Koran (see Qu'ran: below).

Galilee: the northern area of Palestine, where Jesus lived.

Gospels: these are the four short books written by the evangelists in which are related the work, sayings and death of Jesus. In the Bible they appear as "The Gospel According to Saint Matthew", "... to St Mark", etc. These books are frequently referred to in later chapters, and are referrerd to simply as Matthew, Mark, Luke and John. In this book. when reference is to the persons, not to the gospels, their names are preceded by S. (Saint): S.Matthew, S.Mark, S.Luke and S.John. References to texts from the gospels are usually abbreviated to Mtt, Mk, Lk and Jn. Numbers following these names are the chapter and the first verse of the passage referred to, thus "Mtt 2,27" means: "gospel according to S.Matthew, Chapter 2, from verse 27".

Herod: the name of several rulers in Palestine about the time of Jesus.

Herod Antipas: see Antipas.

Herod the Great: born c.73BC; was appointed Governor of Galilee by Julius Caesar in 43BC. Became King of the Jews (Judea) in 40BC and was crowned in 37BC. An able but cruel ruler. That he was indeed the "slaughterer of the innocents" as recorded by Matthew (2,16) is in keeping with his character and with the infighting for power among those near him. He ruled at the time Jesus was born, and died in 4BC.

Herod of Chalcis: a grandson of Herod the Great, brother of Agrippa I (see above), whom he succeeded in AD44. Died AD48.

Holy Shroud of Turin: a length of cloth on which it is believed the body of Jesus lay after the crucifixion; it was drawn up over his head to cover the body, and fumes from the spices used on his body to heal his wounds left an imprint, the closer the contact the darker the print – a sort of negative photograph. Many books have been written about it and there are good reasons to believe it is genuine in spite of a somewhat suspect carbon dating, the result of which declared it a medieval forgery.

Israel, Israelites: originally Israel was used to mean the Hebrew people, who were all Israelites; later when Palestine was divided it became the name of the northern half, and "Israelite" was applied to those Jews living there. The term "Israel" was also applied to the religion of the Jews, and was sometimes used as synonymous with "The People of God". The name Israelite goes back to the younger son of Isaac, Jacob, whose name was changed to Israel. From his twelve sons descended the twelve tribes tribes of Israel who formed the original Hebrew people. But ten tribes revolted and formed a separate kingdom,. In 721BC these were taken into captivity by the Assyrians and in due course became absorbed into the peoples around them, thus becoming the "ten lost tribes of Israel". There remained only two tribes who, at the time of Jesus, inhabited the two adjacent Palestinian kingdoms of Israel and Judah. (See also Jerusalem: below.)

Jerusalem: the capital of Judea in the time of Jesus, founded before 1900BC, and the most important Jewish city in Palestine. The Temple and a palace of Herod were both located there.

Jesus Christ: the name of the eponymous Founder of Christianity, although in reality the orthodox form of Christian doctrine owes more to S.Paul. Strictly speaking "Jesus" (meaning "The Righteous One") was his name and "Christ" was a title, meaning "The Anointed One" – that is, someone appointed to act in God's name. As what we know about Jesus is mainly what is to be found in the gospels, on their accuracy depends our knowledge of Jesus as an historical person.

John the Baptist: appears to have been an Essene, and to have been the mentor of Jesus, whose own mission developed after the Baptist was arrested and executed. (See Antipas, above.)

John the Evangelist: one of the early disciples of Jesus and later an apostle, and the reputed author of the fourth gospel. According to early Christian writers he died at a great age about AD100 at Ephesus (see above).

Joseph: the name of Jesus's nominal father. See Index.

Josephus, Flavius: Jewish historian favoured by the Romans, b.Jerusalem AD37, a few years after the crucifixion. A learned Pharisee. In AD63 sent to Rome as delegate; became Governor of Palestine; found favour with the Romans and after the fall of Jerusalem in AD70 probably lived in Rome. Wrote A History of the Jewish War, Jewish Antiquities, and an Autobiography, covering the years AD37-90. Died some time after AD97.

Judah: around 750BC Palestine was divided into two Jewish kingdoms, Judah in the South, which later became Judea (see below), home of the Jews, and Israel in the north, which later formed Galilee and Samaria. Hence the term "Israelite" at the time of Jesus referred mainly to Jews of Samaria.

Judaism: the religion and customs of the Jews, especially those of Judea.

Judas Iscariot: the disciple of Jesus who betrayed him to the Romans. The name "Iscariot" may come from "Sicarii", the name given to the more militant of the revolutionary-minded Zealots. His betrayal of Jesus would be explained by his belief that Jesus was too pacific to e the new Messiah.

Judea or **Judaea:** the southern area of Palestine. It was governed by a Roman Procurator (or Prefect) from AD6 to AD41, and thus was a Roman Province during most of the lifetime of Jesus. Jerusalem and Bethlehem were both in Judea. See also Pilate.(below) and Archelaus (above).

Koine: the form of Greek used generally in the Roman Empire at the time of Jesus. It was the language of the Jews of the Greek Diaspora and the language of the gospels and other writings in the New Testament.

Koran: see Qu'ran, below.

Luke: see Evangelists, (above).

Mark: supposed author of the gospel which bears his name; traditional founder of the Christian church in Alexandria. (See Evangelists, above.)

Mary: the name of several women in the gospels, amongst them Mary, the mother of Jesus (see Virgin Mary, below).

Matthew: reputed author of the first of the gospels as they appear in the New Testament, and an early disciple and apostle of Jesus (see Evangelists, above).

Messiah: has the same meaning as "Christ" (see Jesus Christ, above): the King whose coming the Jews awaited; he was to deliver them from their oppressors-at the time of Jesus, the Romans.

Nazareth: the town in the North of Palestine, in the area known as Galilee, where Jesus was supposed to have his home (but not his birthplace). But it is uncertain whether Nazareth existed at the time of Jesus's birth, though it had appeared by the time the gospels were written (see Nazarene, below).

Nazarene: Nazorean, Nazoraios: all synonymous (and akin with the Arabic word for Christian, Nazorani) was used as an appellation for the early Christians. At the time of Jesus a Nazarene was a holy man, and the word was sometimes applied to the Essenes, especially to an Essene sect living on the east side of the river Jordan some 150 years before the birth of Jesus. An earlier form of the word with much the same meaning was Nazarite, a term that was formerly applied among early Israelites to holy persons with prophetic gifts. Jesus was reputed to be a holy man, a Nazarene. The word has nothing to do with Nazareth, with which, it seems, it later became confused.

Nero: (Claudius Caesar Drusus Germanicus), b. AD37: Roman Emperor AD54; suspected of starting fire of Rome used as excuse for his persecution of Christians AD64; suicide during revolt AD68.

New Testament: the name given to a collection of writings that form approximately the last third of the Bible. It contains the four gospels, followed by a book known as "The Acts of The Apostles", which is really Part Two of Luke's gospel, dealing with the early development and spread of Christianity after the crucifixion of Jesus. A collection of letters follows; these, which form a substantial part of the New Testament, are called the "Epistles", mainly those written by or attributed to S.Paul. Finally there is a rather strange book called "The Apocalypse" or "Revelation". This present book is concerned only with the historical accuracy of New Testament information about Jesus, so reference is made to books other than the gospels only occasionally.

Old Testament: a collection of Jewish writings, written mostly in Hebrew, before the life of Jesus, which together form approximately the first two thirds of the Bible. They do not directly concern us here. They are also considered as sacred writings by the Jews, they were known and used by Jesus: he is said to have frequently referred to them and quoted from them.

Orthodox: means "following the accepted beliefs and customs". Thus there can be orthodox Jews and orthodox Christians and orthodox Muslims and even orthodox spelling. "Orthodox" is also the title given to many of the groups of Christians in the near and middle East: for example, the Russian and Greek Orthodox Churches; but in this book it is mainly used in its sense of "accepted, according to custom" as above, unless the context indicates otherwise.

Palestine: the area where Jesus was born, now largely occupied by the modern state of Israel.

Papias: c.AD70-140. Bishop of Hieropolis, a town in Phrygia, Asia Minor, 100 miles eastward inland from Ephesus (see above). His writings have survived only as extracts in the form of quotations in the works of later writers. May have known S.John.

Papyri: the name given to ancient manuscripts written on a kind of paper made from reeds.

Passover, Feast of: the most important festival of the Jewish religious calendar celebrating the deliverance of the Jews from Egypt. The Jewish date was Nisan 14th, a date around 1 April (the Jewish calendar resulted in some variation when compared with ours, and there was more than one calendar in use). Pilgrims came to Jerusalem for the feast from far and wide. Individuals would undergo ritual "purification" at the Temple in the days immediately before the feast, and then in groups present a lamb as an offering, the blood of which was sprinkled round the foot of the altar. The lamb was then taken away and eaten for the Passover feast by the group. However many of the Essenes did not eat meat, and ate bread instead. The "Last Supper" that Jesus had with disciples was not the orthodox Passover meal as it took place before the Passover (John 13,1), but it may have been the Essene equivalent using a different calendar.

Paul: a well-educated prominent Jew. He first persecuted the followers of Jesus, but later became a follower himself, and a most important apostle (see above). He wrote a number of long religious letters, called "Epistles", which are in the New Testament. He was responsible for the spread of the doctrine that Jesus was divine, that the death of Jesus on the cross was the sufficient sacrifice demanded by God for the forgiveness of sin, including the stain of original sin with which we are all born. His teaching was based on a belief in the bodily resurrection of Jesus. He was almost certainly executed in Rome AD64.

Peter, Simon Peter: One of the first of the followers of Jesus, and their leader. He appears frequently throughout the period covered by the gospels. Crucified, it is said, upside down, in Rome AD67, but there is no substantial evidence that Peter went to Rome. Because, as the "head of the apostles", it was appropriate that he should have gone to the centre of the Roman Empire, and that the bishops of Rome should be the successors of Peter as the first Pope, the belief that this is what happened was widely accepted as fact. It could be true! Two letters in the New Testament are attributed to him, but their real authorship is problematic.

Pharisees: a numerous and powerful Jewish sect. Strict on the outward forms of the rules of religious observance.

Philo Judaeus: born in Alexandria 20-10BC. Of wealthy family and educated in Greek culture, he remained an ardent believer in the superiority of Judaism. His philosophy of the relationship of the Logos ("the Word") seems to have inspired the preface to John (1,1).

Pilate, Pontius: a Roman "Procurator" – local governor – somewhat unwillingly responsible for having Jesus crucified in order to avoid annoying the Sanhedrin, the Council of the Jews (see below). He was appointed in AD26 and relieved of his post in AD36. Although the gospels picture him as weak but not vicious, in practice he was responsible for some very harsh treatment of those under him.

Qumran: fortress-like buildings situated near the north west coast of the Dead Sea. Often stated to have been the home of a monastic community of Essenes, but this belief seems to be erroneously based on the assumption that the Dead Sea Scrolls, found nearby (see above) originated here. There is no evidence to confirm this, and the ruins suggest that it had a military rather than a religious purpose.

Qu'ran or Koran: the holy book of Islam, the religion of the Muslims. It is not, like the Bible, a collection of different writings (books, poems, letters) but one book, dictated during his lifetime by the Prophet Mohammed.

Rabbi: in New Testament times the term was used to address a scholar or teacher; it did not infer that the person so addressed was a professional "clergyman", as it does today.

Sadducees: a comparatively small Jewish sect, but powerful because they had hereditary rights to provide the priests for the Temple in Jerusalem. When Rome took over Judea from Archelaus they were given back their traditional position as the immediate rulers of Jerusalem and the surrounding country, the Roman Procurator usually remaining at Caearea except at times of festivals when many strangers came to Jerusalem. They imposed their authority by means of the Temple Guards. At the time of Jesus's trial the chief priest was Caiphas, and it was normal procedure for Jesus to be "tried" by him; but only the Romans could pronounce a death sentence. Circumstances obliged them to kowtow to the Romans, who effectually decided who should be the Chief Priest. Their "governing body" was the Sanhedrin (see below). They differed on several doctrinal points from the Pharisees: for example, they did not believe in an after-life.

Saint: in Christian practice this is a title put before the name of persons considered to have lived particularly good lives as Christians or to have died for their faith. In the early days of Christianity it was also used as a general term for the members of a Christian group. It is usually abbreviated before names to St or simply S.

Sanhedrin: the highest court and council of the Jews, composed of 71 elders, priests and scribes. The real power was, however, vested in the High Priest and his council, albeit subject to the approval of the Roman Procurator.

Scribe: in general a person who used professionally his ability to read and write. In Palestine at the time of Jesus the term was applied more particularly to scholarly Jews or rabbis (teachers of religion and law), usually Pharisees.

Septuagint: the Greek translation of the Hebrew Old Testament Scriptures (sacred writings) dating from about 250BC, produced in Alexandria by 72 Jewish scholars for Greek-speaking Jews. Latin for 70 is septuaginta, hence the name. Abbreviated to LXX, Roman numerals fo 70.

Simon the Zealot: one of the disciples of Jesus, whose title indicates that he was one of the freedom fighters opposing Roman rule. Named as a disciple in Matthew (10,4), Mark (3,118), Luke (6,13) and Acts (1,13).

Simon Magus, "Simon the Magician": important in Samaria about AD37 due to his practice of sorcery; offered the apostles money for the gifts of the Holy Spirit conferred by them through laying on of hands (ordination) – hence the term "simony" (Acts,

8,9ff). Said to have written books of heresies, and to have murdered Agrippa I.

Synagogue: the place of worship for every Jewish community. The word also applies to the community group itself. The buildings were usually in a prominent position, and the sexes were segregated.

Therapeutae or **Therapeuts:** monastic Essenes with special gifts in healing, from whom Jesus may have acquired his healing skills, which, in turn, may have come from the Essenes in Egypt, who had acquired it from Buddhist monks who settled there some three hundred years before the birth of Jesus (see above: Alexandria).

The Temple: the central place of worship for Jews in Jerusalem. At the time of Jesus it was an imposing building with several courtyards surrounded by walls. The Temple at the time of Jesus was the third to be erected, largely built by Herod the Great from 50BC, but was only completed seven years before its destruction in AD70. Although Jesus is said to have foretold that "no stone would remain upon another", in actual fact part of the Temple has survived to the present day.

Virgin Mary: the title usually given to Mary the Mother of Jesus, though not in the gospels. More about Mary's role and status is discussed in Chapter VI.

Zealots: a group of Jews actively engaged in opposition to the rule of Rome (see above: Simon the Zealot).

2
Dates

The following dates fit in with available information, but some are more certain than others. Notes are given to suggest degree of accuracy. Dates given as "known" are those widely (though not always universally) accepted as accurate. The assessment of the accuracy of other dates is that of the present writer.

Note that dates BC (Before Christ) go in reverse order: that is 5BC is earlier than 4BC.

Early historians do not always give events in chronological order. Thus the Jewish historian Josephus, when mentioning the Romans' punitive attack on the Arab king Aretas, which happened in AD37, describes immediately before it the events that led up to it – the abandonment by the Jewish ruler Herod Antipas of Aretas's daughter, to whom he was married (see Aretas above), the denunciation of his behaviour by John the Baptist, and the consequent execution of the Baptist by Antipas.. These events are all placed after the death in AD33 or 34 of Philip, the half brother of Herod Antipas and original husband of Herodias. The punishment of Aretas is thus explained by events that happened several years earler, clearly before the death of Philip in AD33/4 though reported after it. It is clear that Josephus kept the series of dependent events together and the whole series, regardless of the actual date indivdual events occurred, was inserted in the form of one complete "story" in thehistorical position that belonged to the final event.

Very early dates are necessarily somewhar speculative.

ca. 1000BC	David King of Israel, followed by Solomon.
ca. 700BC	Israelites taken in captivity to Nineveh.
586BC	People of Judah taken in captivity to Babylon
538BC	Return of some of the Jews to Palestine.

520-515BC	Rebuilding of the Temple in Jerusalem.
509BC	Traditional date for founding of Rome.
480BC	Death of Buddah.
332BC	Palestine conquered by Alexander the Great.
c.300BC	Egypt rules Palestine.
198BC	Syrian rule of Palestine.
63BC	Judea conquered by Romans under Pompey (known).
37-4BC	Herod the Great king (known).
31BC	Roman general Octavian (born 63BC) supreme over Rome.
27BC	Octavian becomes Caesar Augustus, founds Roman Empire.
47BC	Herod the Great appointed Governor of Galilee by Julius Caesar.
40BC	Herod the Great elevated to King of Judea (known).
8 or 7 BC	Birth of Jesus (speculative). Time of year not known: most likely in Spring (not 25 Dec).
8BC-AD33	Mainly unkown years of the life of Jesus.
4BC	Death of King Herod of Judea (known). Herod's son Archelaus became ethnarch (administrator) of Judea, Samaria and Idumea. He was deposed in AD6 for his tyranny.
AD1	Follows immediately after end of 1BC. No year "0".
AD6	Census under Quirinius (Crenius). (Luke 2,2).
AD6	Archelaus, son of Herod the Great, dismissed (known) Antipas, another son of Herod, tetrarch of Galilee and Peraea, and after AD6 of Judea and Samaria. Banished AD39. (known) (See also List of Names.)
AD14	Death of Augustus; start of reign of Emperor Tiberius (known).

AD26	Pontius Pilate appointed Procurator of Judea (known).
AD29-31	S.John the Baptist preaches and baptizes Jesus (probable).
AD30-32	Start of Jesus's ministry (probable).
AD33	Crucifixion of Jesus: at Passover, 3rd April. (The most probable date, but some think AD30 or other near date).
AD34	Death of S.Stephen, the first Christian martyr (assumed).
AD35	Conversion of S.Paul (probable).
AD36	Pilate dismissed. Recalled to Rome arriving after ...
AD37	... death of the Emperor Tiberius. Birth of Nero (all known). Holy Shroud of Turin taken to Edessa (recorded).
AD43	Roman invasion of Britain (known). (Julius Caesar had landed in BC54 but did not remain).
AD49	First Christian Council in Jerusalem (known). Expulsion of Jews and Christians from Rome in 9th year of Claudius (41-54AD) (known).
AD50	First Epistle (letter) of S.Paul and therefore first of the "books" of the New Testament to be written (possible).
AD54	Nero becomes Emperor (known).
AD61	Boudicca (better known as Boadicea), tribal Queen of the Iceni in East Anglia, rebelled unsuccessfully against the Romans (known).
AD64	Fire of Rome (known). Death of S. Paul in Rome during the Emperor Nero's persecution of Christians (very probable).
AD66	Start of Jewish uprising.
AD67	S.Peter martyred in Rome (traditional).

AD68	Death (suicide) of Nero (known).
AD69	Vespasian elected Emperor by Roman army in Palestine (known).
AD70	Destruction of Jerusalem, after Jewish uprising, by the Romans under Titus, son of Emperor Vespasian (known).
AD79	Titus Emperor (known)
AD81	Domitian Emperor (known).
AD93/6	Persecution of Christians under Domitian (known).
AD96	September: Emperor Domitian assassinated (known). Date of first surviving Christian writing other than those in the New Testament, called "The First Epistle of S.Clement", a priest in Rome (assumed).
AD98	Date of writing of the last of the four gospels (John) (earliest; possibly year or two later).
AD100	Death of S.John, last of the apostles to die; and also death of Josephus, Jewish historian (both dates approximate).
AD100	End of "First Century".
AD101-200	"Second Century".
AD324	Constantine the Great made Christianity the official religion of the Roman Empire.
AD397	Council of Carthage settled Canon of New Testament.

BIBLIOGRAPHY

All the books mentioned below have been consulted, some more, some less, during the writing of this book.

The Greek New Testament, Bible Societies, 3rd Edition, German Bible Society, Stuttgart, 1983. Besides the Greek text gives valuable cross references, alternative readings, manuscript sources, etc.

A Reader's Greek-English Lexicon of the New Testament and a Beginner's Guide for the Translation of New Testament Greek, Sakae Kubo, T. & T. Clarke, Ltd., Edinburgh, 1986 impression. Besides saving time looking up words in a dictionary gives valuable word-counts of each book and a useful potted guide to Greek Grammar.

The Holy Bible, New International Version, International Bible Society, New York, 1974.

Nøgle til det Nye Testamente, Peter Schindler, Arne Frost-Hansens Forlag, Copenhagen, 1953. Excellent extensive scholarly commentary from a Catholic standpoint. Reasoned arguments for dates and authorship of all New Testament texts.

Good News For Modern Man, The New Testament in Today's English Version, Fontana Books, Collins, London, 1974 impression. Useful sub-headings make it easy to find events, parables, etc; good index and informative explanation of terms, names etc. Poor translation.

The Four Gospels, Translation by E.V.Rieu, Penguin Classics, Harmondsworth, Middlesex, 1952. Easy to read scholarly translation and good introduction to gospels.

The Evolution of the Gospel, New Translation of the First Gospel with Commentary, J.Enoch Powell, Sometime Fellow of Trinity College, Cambridge, etc. Yale University Press, New Haven and London, 1994. Especially valuable for the way it shows how the first gospel came to be built up. Scholarly translation and commentary on use of words, etc.

Everyman's Encyclopaedia, Third Edition, J.D.Dent & Co., London, 1953. Good general knowledge: includes many articles connected with subjects dealt with in this book. Out of date on some points.

Encarta 95, Microsoft Multimedia Encyclopedia. Contains some useful relevant articles.

Catholic Encyclopedia, Edited by Rev. Peter M.J.Stravinskas, Ph.D., S.T.L. Our Sunday Visitor Inc, Indiana, 1991. Modern Catholic view on some subjects. Not as complete as could be expected. Difficult to use as there are no headers

The Catholic Encyclopedic Dictionary, Edited by Donald Attwater, Cassel & Company, London, 1930. More complete than the above although not so up to date on some points.

Apologetics and Catholic Doctrine, The Most Rev. M. Sheehan, D.D. M.H.Gill & Son Ltd. Fourth Revised Edition, Dublin, 1953. Traditional Catholic teaching.

Early Christian Writings, Translated by Maxwell Staniforth, Penguin Classics, Harmondsworth, Middlesex, 1984 reprint. Does not include any apocryphal gospels.

What Can We Know About Jesus? Howard Clark Kee, Cambridge University Press, 1990.

The World of Jesus, First Century Judaism in Crisis, John Riches, Cambridge University Press, 1990. Useful background information.

Jesus The Man, Barbara Thiering, Corgi Books Edition, London, 1993. A very clever and original treatment of the available material. Ignores India. Difficult to take seriously.

A Search For The Historical Jesus, Professor Fida Hassnain, Gateway Books, Bath, 1994. A sympathetic and scholarly study by a Muslim writer. Very useful for information about Jesus in India. Contains remarkable coloured portrait of the face of Jesus originating from the image on the Shroud of Turin.

The Historical Figure of Jesus, Professor E.P.Sanders, Alan Lane, The Penguin Press, 1993. A scholarly, thorough and informative srudy of the life and times of Jesus, of the gospels and other contemporary testimony.

The Jesus Conspiracy: The Turin Shroud and the Truth about the Resurrection, Holger Kersten & Elmar R. Gruber, English Edition published by Element Books Ltd, Shaftesbury, Dorset, 1994. A very detailed study of the Holy Shroud of Turin, its history and authenticity, and the "resuscitation" of Jesus.

Jesus Lived In India, Holger Kersten, English Edition published by Element Books Ltd., Shaftesbury, Dorset, 1995 Reprint. Contains much of the findings of the above book, but concentrates on the evidence for Jesus in India.

The Jesus Papyrus, Carsten Peter Thiede & Matthew D'Ancona, Weidenfield and Nicholson, London, 1996. Full discussion on Magdalen Matthew fragments and Cave 7 Mark fragment.

The Dead Sea Scrolls In English, G.Vermes. Third, revised edition, Penguin Books, London, 1990.

The Dead Sea Scrolls Deception, Michael Baigent and Richard Leigh, Corgi Books, London, 1992 reprint.

Our Bible and the Ancient Manuscripts, Sir Frederic Kenyon, Eyre and Spottiswoode, London, 1951. A standard work on this subject.

Everyday Life in New Testament Times, A.C.Bouquet, Batsford, London, 1954. Useful historical information.

The Bible as History, Werner Keller, translated by William Neil, Hodder & Stoughton, London 1958. Valuable work on this subject.

Dead Sea Scrolls: "A Closed Book Again", article in The Times, 9 Aug 1995 by Norman Hammond, Archaeological Correspondent. Qumran not an Essene monastery.

INDEX

Page numbers followed by AP = special paragraph in appendix. ff = and following pages and usually refers to the main treatment of the subject.

Abraham 135AP
accuracy (historical) of gospels 31ff, 109, 110
Acts of Apostles 7. 45ff, 118, 123
Adam 8, 127
Agrippa I & II 135AP
Alexander the Great 14, 16, 64
Alexandria 42, 43, 44, 70, 120
aloes 97/98, 100
Antioch 45
angels 52, 72/73, 80, 135AP
Antipas (Herod) 66, 90
apochrypha 51/52, 106
Apostles 5, 11, 136AP
appearances after crucifixion 102/103
Arabia 16
Aramaic texts 24, 25, 35, 41, 112
archaeology 12
Archelaus (Herod) 15, 66, 71, 75, 76, 136AP, dates 150
Aretas IV 136AP
Arimathea, Joseph of 78, 83, 94, 95, 102
ascension 103, 106
astrology, astronomy 67, 68
atonement 8, 85
Babylon 14, 67
Bacon, Roger 60
Barabbas 90
Barnabas, gospel of 23, 51, 52
Benedict, St. 131; Rule of 132
Bethlehem 20, 65, 70, 72, 75, 136AP
Bethany 102, 106
Bible 28, 88, 136AP
birth: stories, 39, 46, 63ff, date of 68
bishop 6, 121
blood and water 93
Britain 16, 79, 151
Buddhism 76, 113, 114, 115
Buddhists 53, 78, 118
Caesarea 19, 42
Caiphas 137AP; see also chief priests
Cana, miracle at wedding 49, 57
Canaanites 13
Canon of New Testament 9, 23, 136AP
Capernaum 21
carbon dating 100
celibacy 117
census 72, 75, 159
centurion 94, 105
chief priests 66, 116; see also High Priest 17, Caiphas 137AP
Chinese astrology 68
Christianity 109, 118; today 121ff, 137AP
Christmas, traditional 64/65
Christ (title of) 1, 125
Church 137AP, early 16, 29
evolution of 8, modern 123ff,
Catholic 99, 123, 124 Eastern Orthodox 123/124 Anglican/Protestant 123, 124

Church of England 128/129
Cleopatra 70
codex 26
Constantine 8
Cornwall 79
Council of Carthage 23
crucifixion 5, 63, 83, 85ff, 137AP; date 151 described, 88/89; surviving, 94
Damascus 6, 16
date of gospels 34, 35/36, 46, 152
David 18, 65, 69/70, 79/82, 95, 137AP, date 149
Dead Sea Scrolls 80, 110/111, 138AP
demons 54
Diaspora 138AP
disciples 11, 119, 138AP
early sources 35
Ebionites 119/120
Edessa 68
editing, early 29, 36, 37, 120
Egypt 13, 14, 15, 41, 53, 66, 70, 75
Elijah 119
Elizabeth 74, 121
Emmaus, disciples of 44, 46, 102
end of world, belief in (eschatology) 36, 80
Ephesus 138AP
epistles (of Paul) 31, 123, date of first 151
Essenes 7, 18, 20, 43, 53, 69ff, 110, 113, 118, 139AP writings of 45, 111, 112 Passover of 90 and crucifixion 95
Euphrates 68
Eusebius 42, 139AP

evangelists 11, 13, 19, 139AP
fatherhood of God 114AP
festivals 17; see also Passover
flight into Egypt 41, 66, 70, 75
forgiveness of sins 8
Gabriel 72, 139AP
Galilee 3, 13, 14, 16, 17, 20, 90, 92, 112, 139AP
Galileo 99
Gamaliel 5, 7
gardener 98
geneaology of Jesus 41, 81, 121
Glastonbury 78
God, gender of 3/4, 114
glorified body: see risen body
gospels 11, 13, 23ff, 139AP; date of 34, 152 authors of 34 order of 37 purpose of 50
Greek language 16, 24
Greek philosophy 9, 63
Gruber, Elmar R. 99
guards at tomb 98
Hassnain, Professor 78, 100
Heaven 104
Hebrews 13
Hebrew language 28, 35, 39, 77, 113
Hellenic (Greek) culture 9, 14, 20, 45, 64
Herod, title 139AP
Herod Chalcis 139AP
Herod the Great 17, 65, 71, 74, 139AP, dates 150
High Priest 17; see also chief priests; Sanhedrin
Holy Index 99
Holy Shroud 141AP, early dates of 151, see also shroud

Idumaea 14
incarnation 8, 74, 119
India 78, 81, 106
innocents, slaughter of 41
Israel, modern 13
Israel, Israelites 13, 16, 80, 141AP
Jainism 113
James 6, 51, 118, 119, 121
  gospel of 23
Jericho 70
Jerusalem 13, 14, 17, 43, 46, 75/76, 90, 91, 102, 104, 119, 141AP destruction of 36
Jesus, birth 39, 46, 63ff, 121, see dates 151 early years 3, 17, 41, 75/76; apocryphal stories 55/56 and Essenes 19, 69/76, 110, 117, 118; divinity of 63, 81 in John 57; miracles to support 61/62; man of God 109; celibacy 117; Nazarene 117/118; portrait 111/112; personality 112, 114/116; ministry of 31, 77, 82; orthodox Jew 17, 75, 114; teaching of 9, 10, 22, 33, 38, 82, 109ff, 126; temptation of 39; crucifixion of: see also Jesus Christ 141AP
Jews 17, 75, 87, 88, 107, 119; see also Hebrews, Israelites
John, St. 11, 46, 119, 141; at crucifiction 91,93
John, gospel of 33, 47ff, 51; date 152AP; prologue 49, 63/64 ending 49; early fragment of 26
John the Baptist 74, 81
John the Presbyter 49/50

Jordan, river 18
Joseph (father of Jesus) 21, 41, 69/78
Joseph of Arimathea: see Arimathea
Josephus Flavius 12, 13, 74, 94, 142AP
Judaism 141AP
Judah 14, 142AP
Judea 13, 14, 15, 66, 71, 74, 142AP
Kashmir 103, 113, 115, 118
Kepler 74
Kersten 99, 103
King of Jews 82
Kingdom of God 49, 79/82
Kings, three 66/67
Koine 16, 45, 77, 112, 117, 143AP
Koran 87, 117, 143AP
Last Supper 9, 48
Latin 16
Law of Moses 18, 119
Lazarus 80
legs broken at crucifiction 92
Levi (Matthew) 40
Lourdes, miracles at 58/59, 61
Luke, St. 11, 63/64, 72, 74, 102
Luke gospel of 35, 45ff, 63/64, 73/75, 91, 102
Magnificat 46, 73
Mark, St. 11, 42/43, 98
Mark, gospel of 42ff, 91; beginnings 63; endings 44; early fragment of 27
Mary, the name 143AP
Mary, Virgin 8, 11, 15, 46, 65, 69ff, 105, 107, 118; see also Virgin Mary 143AP

Mary Magdalene 95, 98, 115
Mass (service of) 9, 48
Mataria 70
Matthew, St. 11, 32/33, 63/64, 69, 127
Matthew, gospel of 39ff, 91, 115; early fragments of 27, 40
Messiah 1, 12, 18, 143AP
Michael, Archangel 80
Middle Ages 61, 87, 120
mind and matter 60
miracles 38, 52, 53ff; as used by Jesus 56; miracles and faith 60; as used by gospels 61, 62; in Acts 62
Mohammed 117
Mosaic Law 18, 119
Mount of Olives 106
Muree 104
myrrh 97
Nabataeans 16
Nativity 63ff; date of 66; see also birth
Nazarene 21, 112, 117, 118
Nazareth 20, 118, 143AP
Negev 16
Nero 2, 143AP; date 152
New Testament 7, 113, 143AP
Nicodemus 83, 96, 102
nunc dimittis 46
Old Testament 14, 41, 142AP
Oracles of the Lord 39, 40
orthodox, meaning 144AP
oral tradition 34
original sin 8
original texts 25
Pakistan: see India
Palestine 12/14; Map 134

Papacy 124
Papias 39, 40, 42, 145AP
papyrus 25; fragments 26; papyri 27, 145AP
parables 20, 38
Paradise 105; see also Heaven
parchment 25
Passover 18, 145AP
Paul (Saul) 5ff, 23, 31, 42, 45, 48, 49, 62, 63, 85, 87, 102, 105, 107, 118, 120, 124, 132, 145AP; date 151
Perea 14, 15
Persia 14, 22
Peter 11, 42, 43, 44, 45, 49, 119, 123/124, 145AP; date 151
Pharisees 6, 18, 83, 146AP
Philip, apocrypha 51, 106
Philistines 13
Philo Judaeus 120, 146AP
Phoenicia 16, 79
Pilate, Pontius 15, 82, 116, 145AP
Pompey 14
Powell, J. Enoch 37, 87
Procurator 17
"Q" sources 35
quelle 35
Qumran 128, 146AP
Quirinius 75; date 150
quotations from gospels, early 27
Rabbi 112, 146AP
Reformation 128
resurrection 85ff; and St. Paul 105
resuscitation 85, 99/100
risen body 101
Roman Army 15, 77/78
Roman coin on Shroud 100
Roman Empire 5, 8, 14, 27

Rome 43, 45/46
Sabbath 92, 97
Sadducees 17, 18, 76, 147AP
Saint, title 147AP
Samaria 14, 16, 116
Samaritans 16, 116
Sanhedrin 147AP; see also chief priests and High Priests
Sathya Sai Baba 112
Saul (later Paul) 6/7 see also Paul
scribe 147AP
Scriptures 130, 131
Sea of Galilee 13, 21
Second Coming 95
sedile 89
Sepphoris 21, 70
Septuagint 24, 147AP
shared sources 41/42
shepherds 72/73
shroud 98; of Turin 98/100, 104, 111; see also Holy Shroud 140AP
Sidon 16, 20
Simeon 46
Simon Magus 148AP
Simon the Zealot 82, 148AP
slaves and slavery 8, 14, 17, 22
Solomon 14
Son of God 7, 119
spear at crucifixion 93
Srinagar 104
Star of Bethlehem 66/67
State occasions 132
stone door of tomb 101
suppedaneum 89
synagogue 148AP
synoptic gospels 34
Syria 6, 15, 16, 21, 75
Teacher of Righteousness 111

Temple, the 14, 17, 75, 76, 87, 114, 148AP
temptation of Jesus 39
therapeutae 46, 54, 148AP
third day 94/95, 97
third millennium 128
Thomas, St. 86, 103, 107
Thomas apocrypha 51; gospel of 55, 106; Acts of 23, 51, 52, 106
Tibet 78, 113
tomb 94, 95, 96/97
transfiguration 119, 120
translations, English 27/29; into Koine (Greek) 28
Trinity, doctrine of 62; see also son of God
truth 128/129
Turin University 100
Tyre 16, 20
versions of gospels, modern: see translations, English
virgin birth 52
Virgin Mary 148AP; see also Mary, virgin
Wicked Priest, the 129
wise men, the three 65/68
women at crucifixion 91, 95, 96
worship 130/131
Zacharias 46, 121
Zeus 113